THE OMELETTE BOOK

THE OMELETTE BOOK

NARCISSA G. CHAMBERLAIN

Drawings by Hilary Knight

DAVID R. GODINE, PUBLISHER
Boston

Published in 1990 by
DAVID R. GODINE, PUBLISHER, INC.
Horticultural Hall
300 Massachusetts Avenue
Boston, Massachusetts 02115

First published in 1955 by Alfred A. Knopf

Library of Congress Cataloging-in-Publication Data

Chamberlain, Narcissa G.
The omelette book / Narcissa G. Chamberlain.
p. cm.
Reprint. Originally published: New York : Knopf, 1956, © 1955.
ISBN 0-87923-842-9
1. Omelets. I. Title.
TX745.C47 1990   89-46182
641.6'754—dc20   CIP

First printing
PRINTED IN THE UNITED STATES OF AMERICA

PREFACE

THE OMELETTE BOOK was published by Alfred A. Knopf in 1955. Mr. Knopf, gentleman giant of the publishing industry, was the personal patron within his company of books on food and cooking, published for his pleasure and with every certainty that profit would follow. In 1981, THE OMELETTE BOOK went into its thirteenth hardcover printing. It was one of many early Knopf cookbooks, choice, true, and modest, that sold for decades. It was published in paperback and had editions in England, Germany, and, wonderfully, in Japan. The book is a classic, a conclusion Alfred Knopf might think superfluous, having made that judgment thirty-five years ago.

The author's daughters are grateful indeed to David Godine and his staff for making the same judgment when rights for re-publication became available. THE OME-LETTE BOOK seems addicted to good publishers.

During the 1950s, Narcissa G. Chamberlain was hard at work collaborating with her husband, the printmaker, photographer, and writer Samuel Chamberlain, on an epic volume, *Bouquet de France: An Epicurean Tour of the French Provinces*, which was to have its own in-print history of more than a quarter century. For a bit of relief from testing the demanding chefs' recipes for that book, she began keeping notes on her home-kitchen emergency meal, the omelette. In the library of cookbooks the Chamberlains had accumulated over the years, she discovered more documentation than one cook or one book could possibly use or need. She determined to make a book, neat and brief, about the usefulness of the omelette—how a bit of this and that in the refrigerator, vegetable bin, or pantry reserves could be used to produce an original dish, every time, on the ancient base, simple but tricky, of a skilletfull of fresh eggs. Of course, extravaganzas also appear—caviar omelettes, the "Cardinal Omelette." Omelettes can travel to any heights, though a perfect one *aux fines herbes* may be the true pinnacle.

Today, the egg is viewed with suspicion. Without a doubt, when you eat eggs nowadays, they had best be good, dressed to perfection and with ease. THE OMELETTE BOOK has a new mission—to see to it that no ration of the wonderful egg is wasted on routine breakfast scrambles.

Narcisse Chamberlain, 1990

CONTENTS

POULTRY AND GAME OMELETTES

MEAT OMELETTES

VEGETABLE OMELETTES

SWEET DESSERT OMELETTES

MISCELLANEOUS OMELETTES

SAUCES

THE CHRONICLE OF
THE OMELETTE

THE CHRONICLE OF
THE OMELETTE

I T IS EASY TO BELIEVE that since there have been eggs
there have been omelettes. The recipe of Apicius, the
Roman epicure and outstanding glutton of his day, is
one of the first recorded. His *ovemele* or eggs with honey (and
pepper, of all things!) may well be the origin of the very
name which distinguishes the omelette to this day.

The golden unit of the egg has always been a symbol of
life or subsistence itself, made use of by philosophers, his-
torians, and theologians. The ancients held the egg in a kind
of sacred veneration. It represented the world and the ele-
ments in the shell (earth), white (water), yolk (fire) and
air, which is under the shell.

The connection with Easter may be related to the pagan
spring festival of rebirth, or have a simpler explanation in the
fact that the egg, forbidden during the fasting of Lent, reap-
peared on the menu joyously at Easter. Thomas Aquinas, the
great theologian, uses the egg as a symbol of the unity of life.
And where would we be now if Christopher Columbus had
not been a man with the ingenuity and imagination to set an
egg on its end?

It seems the egg was put to unusual use in Rome by Livia,
wife of the Emperor Augustus. When she was expecting a
child the oracle advised her to carry an egg in the warmth of
her corsage, and the sex of her child would be indicated by
whether a male or female chick was hatched in this cozy nest.

Within three weeks a young cock emerged and shortly after this Livia gave birth to Tiberius. When the circumstances of this extraordinary event were made known it became a fashionable custom among the matrons of Rome to follow Livia's example. Perhaps this was no more absurd, though surely more uncomfortable, than the many other superstitions regarding this still unsolved problem.

It was once forbidden to destroy the egg by eating, as this palatable protein was regarded only as a potential chicken. Fortunately for us, the worldly old Romans discarded this taboo and prepared eggs accompanied by everything from rose petals to fowls' brains.

Some maintain the omelette's name is derived from *amelette,* meaning blade, transposed through a series of distortions, including *alemette* and *alumette.* This described the long flat shape of the omelette. In certain eighteenth-century English books, whose authors were undoubtedly better cooks than spellers and had a characteristically deaf ear to the subtleties of the French language, there were deviations into *amalet* and *aumlet.* Some of these recipes call for an awkward eighteen to twenty-four eggs.

Ann Cook's *amalet* contains twelve eggs and "half a hundred" of asparagus, later referred to as "grass," even as in the markets of today. This asparagus omelette is "fried a nice brown," turns out to be an inch thick, and is served with vinegar and butter sauce.

Ann Cook's contemporary, Elizabeth Raffald, on the other hand, spells it *aumlet.* But she had her own way with words, and her *Experienced English Housekeeper* contains such remarkable terms as "Pidgeons Transmogarified." She recommends a quarter of a pound of butter to six eggs, a grandiose eighteenth-century extravagance no longer considered necessary.

Probably the most famous name ever associated with the

omelette is that of Mme Poulard, of Mont-Saint-Michel on the
coast of France. She was born Annette Boutiaut and came to
the Mount as servant in the family of the chief architect
charged by the government with the repair and restoration of
the abbey. There she met and later married Victor Poulard,
oldest son of the local baker. The young couple started their
long and successful career as proprietors of the Hôtel Saint-
Michel Tête d'Or. They found the going a little hard in those
early days before the causeway to the mainland was built. Few
pilgrims came to the Mount, which for many years had fallen
into disuse as a religious shrine. As repairs were made and
more and more visitors arrived, M. and Mme Poulard found
themselves swamped upon occasion by crowds of hungry and
impatient travelers who arrived at unexpected moments, depending upon the tides and weather. They had been spotted
by her maids from the ramparts as they approached in car-
riages, their numbers approximated with the aid of binoculars.
It was then that the resourceful and altogether practical and
charming Mère Poulard recognized through simple observa-
tion that the omelette was the answer to her difficulties. It was
quickly made, hot and satisfying. As they approached the
hotel, the travelers were greeted by her warm and motherly
smile, their hunger quickly stilled by the savory omelettes
made before their eyes at the open hearth. Uncertainty of hour
and numbers was no obstacle. The fame of her omelettes
spread. It became a part of the ritual for the guests to stand in
admiring groups at her shoulder to watch her skill with the
long handled skillet. Her secret? She was merely an excellent
cook who used the freshest of local eggs with plenty of the
best butter. The ingredients were no more mysterious than
this. The handling was deft, the eggs moderately beaten, and
the long-handled pan moved continuously back and forth over
the hot coals. "Never let the butter brown in the pan," she
cautioned, "and take care not to overcook the omelette." Of

recent years her descendants, it would seem, have modified the nature of the "Omelette de la Mère Poulard" by the long beating of the eggs to the point of foamy froth. The result is light and of great delicacy, probably neither a corruption nor yet an improvement over the original.

Among the chroniclers of the omelette none has told its story with more wit and charm than Philéas Gilbert, chef, gastronome, author, and friend of Escoffier and Prosper Montagné. His tribute to this paragon of dishes is spiced with anecdote and humor and not unmixed with practical advice.

Listen then, if you will, to the gay M. Philéas Gilbert, his eyes sparkling with humor, his chef's cap perched jauntily on his head:

Depending on the point of view, an omelette may be really nothing, or else it may be grandeur itself. Some explain it in two lines of vulgar prose; others judge it unworthy of their pen; for myself, I would like an entire book to describe it. And to describe the gastronomic merits of the omelette I call to my assistance the full support of the protecting divinities whose shadows hover over the temples of good fare, where their priests officiate—white coiffed and scabbard at side—before altars of glowing coals.

For me, all the seductions of a language of imagery in order to sing of the glories of the omelette! Of the omelette simple or composite, pointed up with herbs, punctuated with bits of ham, or striped with black mourning truffles. Filled with an aristocratic concoction of fish roes and essence of crayfish, or abundantly ornamented with cubes of kidneys steeped in Madeira wine. Simple dish among all, or, at the will of the creator surrounded by extraordinary complexities, capable of attaining to supreme transcendence, to the most luminous heights.

This dish means nothing to you? Profane one that you are!

But I understand. For you the simple omelette is but an ordinary treat, or the hope of a country meal in the course of some rural holiday. And is there really need to have earned one's doctorate in cookery in order to turn out an omelette? Eggs improved with a dash of salt and pepper, tossed into bubbling butter and there you are! In fact that *is* all there is to it, but try it to see how it goes—in a new saucepan! And would you know how to distinguish the exact degree of coagulation of the albumin in order to keep it drooling-moist, or to achieve a firmer perfection? To roll it in three, to garnish it skillfully, and to turn it out with one gesture? The fact is, take care, the coagulation is abrupt, the exact degree easily overstepped, and you mightily risk turning out a pretty piece of cardboard in guise of an omelette. In this case, it is no longer an omelette, it is a little projectile good for breaking window panes.

It has long been believed that like happy people, the omelette has no past. But grave scholars affirm it in enumerating the cooking utensils gathered in the ruins of Herculaneum and Pompeii. Others pretend that it figured in the wedding menu of Prince Caranus, or that it is descended from the *ovamellita* (eggs and honey) of the Romans, while there are the stubborn ones who assign its origin to the Renaissance epoch.

With the leave of the savants, I will teach them who the inventor was. It was Lucullus, of gourmand memory, who conceived the idea. And these were not common omelettes, these composed of the eggs of ostriches, pheasants, quail, and ortolans, filled with knowing mincemeats, which he caused to be served. The omelettes of Lucullus surpassed the famous wild boar stuffed with live thrushes of this great gastronomic epoch.

But the Roman Empire crumbled, the torch of civilization was extinguished, the art of good eating fell into desuetude, and there was a return to primitive feasts. The recipe for the omelette would have been forever lost had not the religious orders gathered it in and submitted it for several centuries to new experimental combinations. And when came the Renaissance, the omelette, born of the meditations of Lucullus, leaped the wall of the cloister, became commonly known again through the efforts of monastic cooks, conservators of the great principles and instigators of great precepts, and became later the object of grave discussions of three Councils and the subject of half a dozen papal bulls.

Before the omelette all tastes are admitted, all preferences affirmed, originality surges forth, and depravity itself shows the tip of its ear.

Here the joyous Gascon [1] seats himself at table, the eve of the Battle of Ivry, before an omelette stuffed with garlic; and is concerned with the imprecations fulminated by Horace against the "asphodel," dear to the people of his Béarn.

It is Louis XV, cooking in the small royal apartments, and so engrossed in the execution of an omelette *aux morilles* that he forgot the coffee in preparation,—whence the startled exclamation of la Du Barry, *"La France, ton café f—— le camp!"*

Here is the Duke of Orléans, fastidious and prodigious gourmand, executing at the palace of Fontainebleau an omelette of one hundred and twenty eggs, where extracts and essences, purées and minces, truffles and crayfish raised its cost to the pretty total of 600 francs. Fantastic omelette whose recipe I hold at the service of economical housewives.

Here is the philosopher Descartes seated with neither

[1] Henry IV of France.

disgust nor remorse before an omelette composed of eggs laid eight or ten days before and declaring that he could not understand it otherwise. Let us not quibble with the defunct author of *Treatise on Light* about his strange taste; it had for him the support of the proverb *De gustibus et coloribus.*

A glance in passing upon the succulence of "the tuna fish omelette with combined sauces" invented by a gallant canon in honor of the beautiful Mme Récamier, exalted to the superlative by the dilettante of cookery who was Brillat-Savarin. And one word alone for the omelettes with purée of ham enjoyed in the very middle of Lent by a Prince, high dignitary of the Church, Catholic, apostolic, and Roman.

The golden-robed omelette has also its dramatic page. Condorcet owed to it his arrest and death. It is known how the former President of the Constituent Assembly of 1792, outlawed by the terrorists, came to a miserable end. Trailed and pursued, he stopped one day, gripped by the pangs of hunger, at an inn at Clamart and committed the imprudence of ordering an omelette of twelve eggs. This was enough to render him suspect, and ten minutes later, denounced by his amiable hostess, he was arrested and incarcerated.[2]

USES OF THE OMELETTE

❀ It is a far cry from these dramatic episodes in M. Gilbert's glamorous history of the omelette to the problems of the harried housewife of today. Dishwashers and automatic blenders replace many pairs of hands, but no mechanical voice answers the eternal question "what shall we have for dinner?" If you are a normal busy woman and find mealtimes continually overshadowing the many duties of a crowded day, this was

[2] Philéas Gilbert, "Variations sur l'Omelette" in Alfred Suzanne, *250 Manières d'Accommoder et de Servir les Œufs (Appendix).*

written for you. Are you an inexpert cook and master of no
particular dish? Have you ever been faced with the problem
of your husband's old college classmate appearing on the
doorstep as you are about to sit down to last night's leftovers?
Would you combine economy and quick preparation in one
appetizing whole? The outlook is not as dismal as you think.
The omelette, a half-forgotten and much neglected cooking
classic is ready to come to your rescue. The marvelous versa-
tility of this dish will make you wonder how you ever lived
without it. The enormous range of its possibilities has almost
disappeared from current books on cookery. The omelette has
sunk to the level of just another way to do the breakfast eggs.

ITS ECONOMY AND VERSATILITY

❀   For the appetizing use of leftovers there is nothing to
equal it. For economy in extending small luxuries to their ut-
most it has no peer. Questions of nutrition and balanced diet
are answered by the infinite variety of fillings which may be
enfolded within its warm embrace. Serve omelettes for breakfast, lunch, or dinner. No dish so lends itself to the inventive-
ness of the cook—and with less risk. It is also a common basis
for international understanding, as it were, in the kitchen—
one to which anyone may add the trimmings of his national
imagination. Though the best recipes are basically French (as
what isn't in this field?) the Italian *fritatta,* which has a
friendly open face, is excellent with spinach, small squash,
Parmesan cheese, or white bait. Spain uses various combinations of onion, tomato, mushrooms, and green peppers. The
Chinese may add bean sprouts, shrimps, and mushrooms in
their own delicate and distinctive way. The Russians have used
caviar and sour cream. The modern Frenchman Paul Reboux,
called by professional chefs a vandal and barbarian, by others
a creative genius, recommends a fantasy he calls an "ameliora-
tion" of the classic tomato omelette. Tomato purée is first

blended with the egg yolks, the omelette is further colored with a few drops of carmine and served surrounded by a Creole rice tinted with methyl blue! Only the adaptable omelette could retain a semblance of its original nature under such treatment. As for us, this seems an unnecessary gilding of the lily.

But the aspect of a dish does play its part, and the classic omelette repertoire contains many colors, shapes, and sizes. The Tricolor is really three on one platter, colored respectively by spinach purée, tomato, and cream, each mingled with the eggs before cooking. The fanciful omelette En Galantine looks something like a layer cake made of six separate flat omelettes and five delectable fillings concocted of ham purée, truffles, foie gras, sweetbreads, and mushrooms with cream. No matter that this sensational dish involves six separate bowls for mixing the eggs and as many saucepans for the fillings! Its more bourgeois cousin the Nancéenne is made with two flat omelettes containing onions and chopped parsley, slices of blood sausage between, parsley and brown butter on top. Almost any omelette appreciates a beauty treatment in the form of an encompassing ring of smooth sauce, or a savory filling placed in a slit made on top after the omelette is folded. The Célestine is a pretty dessert composed of a mound of tiny omelettes each filled with delicate apricot jam, the whole sprinkled with powdered sugar and quickly glazed under the broiler.

With all the elaborate interpretations of this favorite dish it is equally important to satisfy the simple appetite with a classic Plain Omelette. Remember that from this basic conception stem all the other relations, rich and poor, of this interesting family. In mastering this one dish alone you establish yourself firmly in the tradition of sound cookery and are fairly on your way to acquiring a flattering reputation. Because, of course, vanity enters honestly into this art as any other, and all creative artists have need of a certain amount of recognition and esteem.

THE BASIC OMELETTE

✿ To instruct you in the making of the plain, or basic, omelette we can do no better than to quote again the sprightly Frenchman, Philéas Gilbert who says:

I would on your behalf mount the chair of the professor and, in my generosity, initiate you into the mysteries of turning out an omelette.

In one hand I brandish the fork of demonstration, in the other I take up my words and use them in these terms: the very maximum number of eggs for a perfect omelette —ten. [Let *us* start with six, ample for three, sometimes enough for four people.] In a bowl a rigorous beating confuses the yolks and whites, salt and pepper within reason. In the pan the butter whimpers, fumes, and crackles. This is the instant, this the moment. The golden liquid of the beaten eggs falls in a spout into the surprised butter and, whirling, the fork assures an even cooking, disaggregates the egg molecules too violently seized by the heat, unifies the mass. . . . On guard! Alert! The left hand lifts the pan as the right hand folds the omelette on the sinister side. One count—and a neat blow on the end of the saucepan handle folds it on the dextral side. Two counts—one upside-down movement finally turns it out upon the platter, impeccably golden and elegantly molded. Rapidly a fragment of butter pierced by the tip of a knife skims the surface leaving a glistening trail. 'Tis done. Behold the classic omelette.

If it is permissible to add to this dramatic recital, it might be noted that thirty seconds beating with the fork is enough, adequate to "confuse" six eggs, that three teaspoons of cold water added to them makes the omelette tender, whereas milk has the opposite effect. The pan should heat gradually on a medium hot fire, never too quickly nor to excess. Test its temperature with a bit of butter on the end of a fork. The butter should definitely sizzle but *not* turn brown. A generous tablespoon is adequate for a six-egg omelette. Spread it by tilting and turning the pan in all directions to coat the surface. When the frothing bubbles of butter have subsided, in go your eggs. Stir just a second or two with the *flat* of the fork. Tilt the pan to run the eggs up and around the sides, and keep the pan moving in a back and forth motion so the omelette remains slipping and free. Lift the edges here and there and allow the more liquid part to run under. If you are not yet expert with M. Gilbert's "neat little blows" on the end of the saucepan handle, fold the omelette simply with a spatula left side to center and while the surface of the eggs is still soft. Then with the right side slipping over the edge of the pan, hold the platter under it in close contact and turn the pan completely over thus accomplishing the third fold neatly.

WARNINGS

❀   This sounds very simple and really becomes so with practice, but the negative side of the picture may as well be included. *Don't* beat your eggs too long and don't use an egg beater. This whacks all the life out of them. They become thin and are tough when cooked. *Don't* heat your pan too quickly nor to the point where the butter browns, lest your omelette stick. At the same time *don't* drop the butter in until it sizzles on contact. *Don't* skimp on your butter, as this may also cause the omelette to stick. A few drops of oil with the butter help avoid this calamity.

THE PAN

❀   The omelette pan must have rounded sloping shoulders to allow the eggs to spread when tilted and to slide easily onto the platter when cooked. It is no mere affectation, but a practical fact that this pan should not be washed, but wiped out with paper after use to preserve the oily surface. It should be reserved for omelettes alone. If particles adhere, rub the surface with coarse salt and a few drops of oil. A new pan, which should be of heavy cast aluminum, or other metal of good weight, may be seasoned by slowly heating oil in it. The pan only improves with use if properly cared for and becomes the jealously guarded treasure of any cook.

The pan must not be too small, nor too large, for the number of eggs. In the first case the omelette will be too thick and you will find it difficult to cook through without toughening the bottom. In the second case the result will be too thin and dry. A pan about nine inches in diameter at the top is right for a three- or four-egg omelette; ten inches to twelve inches in diameter for a six- to eight-egg omelette. Larger than this is hard to handle and it is safer to make a pair of omelettes for one meal than to attempt a very large one. A tiny pancake size pan is used for a one-egg omelette or for the small ones made in series as the Célestine.

THE EGGS

❀ Eggs seem to pass through three stages in the beating. Thirty seconds of brisk work with a fork is usually sufficient to blend four to six eggs. More than this tends to take all the joy out of them, as we have stated. A *much* longer beating brings them around again to the frothy stage and produces a fine creamy omelette but it must never be overcooked. Needless to say, we deal only with the first and last of these three stages. When yolks and whites are beaten long and separately, then reunited quite completely, sometimes accompanied by cream, sugar, liqueurs, and generous quantities of butter, we are getting into the higher realms of omelette making, the Mousseline or soufflé omelette desserts. Never do we consider that depraved form, sometimes known as the "fluffy" omelette, where yolks and whites are beaten separately, never completely remarried, the whites drying stiffly within the yellow folds. The result is a sort of soft chamois cushion stuffed with cotton wool.

After the impeccably fresh eggs and the best quality butter, the other ingredients of a good omelette are practice, for which there is no substitute, the ideal pan, and a generous dash of self-confidence.

With the basic omelette well in hand you will want to try some of the many possible variations. (Always prepare the fillings and sauces first, turning out the omelette itself just before serving.) Some of the most delicious are the simplest to prepare, containing either ham, fresh herbs, mushrooms, cheese, or onions. With flowering ambition you will want to try a filling which puts the omelette in the category of a main-course dish; or a dessert omelette as a heavenly liqueur-scented finale to a good dinner. Your choice is wide, the list is long, and we hope you will agree with M. Gilbert that the omelette of distinguished history deserves a book of its own.

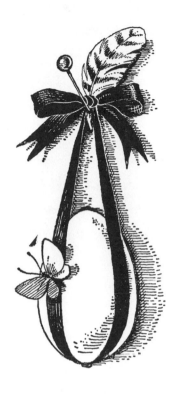

T HE FOLLOWING RECIPES *have been grouped under "Basic Omelettes" and general chapter headings resembling the order of courses of a meal. Under each chapter heading is an alphabetical listing dictated by the chief ingredients involved. The basic omelettes should be mastered first as it seems unnecessary to repeat these instructions in the recipes that follow.*

If you have the remnants of a ham or roast, one or two chicken livers, or a cupful of cold vegetables in your refrigera-

tor, *a quick glance at the appropriate heading in the chapters "Meat," "Poultry and Game," or "Vegetables" will show a variety of delicious ways to utilize these ingredients.*

You may want a hearty breakfast omelette, a main lunch dish, or a light fish course to precede the roast. All may be found here in great variety. And have you ever considered small cold omelettes with savory fillings to replace the monotonous starchy sandwich for a picnic? Or a more elaborate one like the Cambacérés (see Miscellaneous Omelettes, page 162) for a cold buffet? Serve the German omelette, rolled and cut in sections, with roast meat in place of Yorkshire pudding or potatoes.

It is almost too obvious to mention that many of the fresh ingredients here described, such as clams, lobster and crab meat, tomato sauce, vegetables, and other things, may be replaced by good canned varieties.

Whatever your need may be, the omelette is your dish.

BASIC OMELETTES

BASIC OMELETTES

PLAIN OMELETTE

✿ *Before making the plain omelette it would be wise to read the detailed instructions in the introductory chapter.* Break 6 eggs into a bowl, add 3 teaspoons of cold water, ¼ teaspoon of salt, a pinch of freshly ground pepper, and beat with a fork (not a mechanical beater) for 30 seconds. (If it is to be a dessert omelette, add 2 tablespoons of sugar to the eggs and no pepper.) Heat the omelette pan until the butter sizzles at the touch, melt 1 generous tablespoon of butter in the pan, and pour in the eggs. Stir once or twice with the flat of the fork, lift the edges as the eggs begin to cook, and let the liquid part run under. Shake the pan back and forth to keep the omelette free. When cooked but still soft on top, turn the left side to the center, slide the omelette well to the right edge of the pan, and turn out in three folds on the platter.

MOUSSELINE OMELETTE

✿ *This is an extraordinarily creamy, delicate, and delicious way of preparing an omelette and not to be confused with the so-called "fluffy" omelette, in which the separately beaten yolks and whites of the eggs are not afterwards mixed together, and which usually results in a dry and tasteless concoction. The mousseline omelette, on the contrary, is particularly palatable in texture and flavor because of the blending of the beaten eggs and the proc-*

ess of cooking with a good quantity of butter, and sometimes added cream. This method may be used instead of the standard plain omelette with almost any of the fillings or accompaniments described in this book and is particularly suitable for sweetened dessert omelettes, whether served with rum, fruit in various forms, nuts, or other combinations. You have the advantage of economy also, as 4 or 5 eggs make the show of more in bulk.

Separate the yolks from the whites of 4 eggs and beat the yolks well until pale and thick, with salt, pepper, and 1 tablespoon of cream. (4 yolks to 3 whites makes a particularly rich combination preferred by some.) Beat the whites until stiff but not dry. This means just until they stand up in peaks, *no* more. Mix yolks and whites delicately together until blended. Melt 2½ tablespoons of butter in an omelette pan and when sizzling, pour in the eggs, stirring with a spoon and bringing the outer edges in toward the center until they begin to take on a certain consistency. Cook rather slowly and shake the omelette in the pan with a horizontal back-and-forth motion to avoid sticking. The whole thing should remain creamy and light and not be over-cooked. Plenty of butter must be used to avoid sticking to the pan. Fold out double on a platter. Serve plain or with desired filling.

If it is to be a dessert omelette, add 6 tablespoons of sugar, ½ teaspoon of vanilla, ⅛ teaspoon of salt, and of course no pepper, when beating the 4 yolks.

GERMAN OMELETTE

 This resembles a thin pancake, rather than the usual classic omelette, and is made with a batter containing flour and cream, or rich milk. Such an omelette may be spread with a purée of mushrooms or spinach or other

*fine filling, rolled up, and served to accompany a meat
dish. It is also a good accompaniment for a vegetable
dish when rolled up without any filling and sliced in
pieces which are placed around the vegetable on the platter. With sweetenings, it can be used for a fine dessert.*

Put 2 tablespoons of flour in a bowl, stir in, one at a time, 3
whole eggs, beating with a whisk, and add ½ cup of cream,
or whole milk. Season with salt and pepper and a little grated
nutmeg. Stir until smooth. Melt 1 teaspoon of butter in a pan
and pour in half the batter to make a *very* thin omelette, or
pancake. Keep the heat moderate, and, when slightly browned
on one side, slide the omelette onto a plate, re-butter the pan,
and turn back to brown a moment on the other side. Slide out
on a plate, then cook the second omelette. These are rolled up
and served side by side on a platter with a little browned butter or meat juice on top. Or they may be cut in sections and
placed around a platter of meat or vegetables. For other uses
see following chapters.

ITALIAN FRITTATA

The ingredients for the frittata are the same as for the classic
plain omelette, though if filling is used, instead of being
folded into the center of the omelette it is mixed with the eggs
before pouring them into the pan. This omelette is about
½-inch thick and served flat and round instead of folded.
Sometimes it is cooked on one side only, until the eggs are
set. If you wish to cook it on both sides, turn it by placing a
plate upside down over the omelette when almost cooked and,
holding plate and pan closely together, turn the pan quickly
upside down over the plate. The omelette can then be slipped
back into the pan from the plate, cooked side up. An easier
method is to put it briefly under a hot broiler.

When vegetables or other ingredients are left in the pan in which they are cooked, the eggs poured over them, mixed and cooked therewith, it is necessary to serve this from the pan, as the mixture practically always sticks a little. In Florence and some parts of Italy this is called a *tortino*. It is usually cooked in individual two-handled gratin dishes and served forthwith.

OMELETTE FONDANTE

This is the classic plain omelette but made with 1 tablespoon of cream and fragments of butter (about 1 tablespoon for 4 to 6 eggs) added to the beaten eggs. As they cook, the bits of butter melt into little pockets of added richness and flavor.

OMELETTE SOUFFLÉ

The soufflé omelette is a dessert and is prepared in the same manner as a soufflé, the chief difference being that the eggs are cooked in an oval shallow baking dish resembling an omelette in form. The chief distinction between the soufflé omelette and the mousseline omelette is that the soufflé omelette contains extra egg whites and is cooked in the oven, whereas the mousseline omelette contains an equal number of yolks and whites (or even one extra yolk, if desired) and is cooked on top of the stove. This omelette takes less time to cook than the true soufflé, not being as deep. It is well to keep a little of the mixture apart in order to decorate the top by means of a pastry bag with rosettes or other designs before placing in the oven. If one does not wish to be so elaborate, the omelette may be smoothed with a spatula into the form of an oval mound, higher in the center and marked with a lengthwise depression or slit. This omelette may be flavored with vanilla, almond extract, grated lemon or orange rind, chocolate, rum, kirsch, or other liqueurs. The baking should be done in a moderately hot oven and, just before it is completely cooked, sugar evenly sprinkled over the surface through a fine sieve. The omelette is then returned to the oven to acquire a light golden glaze. An even larger proportion of whites is used to top the Omelette Norvégienne *(see Dessert Omelettes, page 149), sometimes called* Omelette Soufflé Surprise, *which resembles the Baked Alaska and is the most impressive of elaborate and showy desserts—also one of the most truly delicious.*

The recipe given here is for the simple sweet soufflé omelette flavored only with vanilla. For other flavorings see Sweet Omelettes, *page 136.*

Mix 4 egg yolks, ½ cup of granulated vanilla-flavored sugar, and a pinch of salt. Beat the mixture well until it has become pale-lemon colored and thick enough to flow in a "ribbon" from the spoon. This means really thick, practically like a mayonnaise. Beat 6 egg whites until stiff but not dry and fold carefully into the yolks as for a soufflé. Butter an oval shallow baking dish or oven-proof platter and drop the mixture all at once onto it, reserving a little for decorating if desired. With a spatula smooth the eggs into an oval mound, form rosettes or other decoration with a pastry tube. (A name or initials are good for a birthday party.)

It is less handsome but equally delicious if just marked with a lengthwise slit, about ½-inch deep at the high center of the omelette, when partly cooked. Cook about 10 minutes in a 300° pre-heated oven. Sprinkle granulated sugar evenly over the top through a fine sieve, make the slit along the top and spread it open, turn the oven to its hottest, and glaze the omelette for 5 minutes. You will find your decoration or initials standing out in pretty golden relief. This omelette should be creamy and not over-cooked.

SEAFOOD OMELETTES

SEAFOOD OMELETTES

ANCHOVY   **OMELETTE NIMOISE**
(Anchovy filets, garlic)

❁ *All the aroma of Provence is contained in this simple omelette.*
Prepare 6 eggs for a plain omelette and add 6 anchovy filets, finely chopped, with the other seasoning. Rub the bowl with garlic before beating the eggs and cook the omelette with 1 tablespoon of olive oil instead of butter.

ANCHOVY   **ANCHOVY OMELETTE AU CROUTONS**
(Bread, anchovies)

❁ *A sandwich with the bread in the middle, for a change.*
Fry 2 halved slices of bread in oil on both sides till slightly browned and crisp. Soak 4 salted anchovies 20 minutes in cold water, drain, dry, split lengthwise in filets, and clean. Or you may use canned filets drained of their oil. Now make 2 thin 2-egg omelettes, do not fold but place flat on a round serving plate. Between them lay the fried toast pieces, upon which you have spread the anchovy filets. Over this round omelette sandwich pour 2 tablespoons of fresh tomato sauce (see page 175) or ½ teaspoon meat extract melted in 3 tablespoons hot stock.

ANCHOVY　　　　　　ANCHOVY PICNIC OMELETTES
(Anchovy butter)

❀ *Do not be put off by this notion of cold omelettes. This one is savory and satisfying.*

Beat 6 eggs as for a plain omelette and spoon out one at a time into a tiny pan to make 4 little flat omelettes cooked on both sides. Cool on a baking sheet. Spread each one with anchovy butter (see page 171). Roll up, wrap in wax paper, and keep in the ice box to be used for a picnic lunch.

CAVIAR　　　　　　　RUSSIAN CAVIAR OMELETTE
(Caviar, sour cream)

❀ *This dish is a series of tiny caviar-filled omelettes and may be served cold as an hors d'œuvre with the vodka (or cocktails, to you) as in Russia, or hot as an entrée, in which case cold sour cream may be passed separately.*

Beat 6 eggs for an omelette with the usual seasoning of salt and pepper, but in this case a rather strong dash of cayenne pepper is added. Make a series of little omelettes in your smallest pan, using about 2 tablespoons of egg mixture for each. Turn each one barely to cook but not brown the upper side. Spread separately on a baking sheet, paler side up, and keep warm. Spread a little Russian caviar on each, fold over, and serve at once with sour cream. The caviar must not be allowed to cook or this ruins it.

If the omelettes are to be served cold, allow them to cool before filling. Red salmon caviar or whitefish caviar may be substituted with good results.

CLAM   ITALIAN CLAM OMELETTE
(Clams, garlic, tomato, onion, herbs)

Wash a dozen clams (either steamers or hard-shell clams will
do) and place in a pan with 2 tablespoons hot olive oil and
½ clove of garlic, chopped. Cover and heat until the clams
are opened. Remove clams from the shells and replace them
in the pan with their juice and oil. Add 2 tablespoons tomato
paste, 1 small onion, finely chopped, and a pinch of orégano
(or 2 tablespoons of tomato sauce) and simmer for 10 to 15
minutes. Beat 4 or 5 eggs as for a plain omelette, adding 1
tablespoon finely chopped parsley to the seasonings. Make a
flat Italian omelette, or *frittata,* cooked on both sides. Slide
onto a round serving dish, pour the clams and sauce over it,
and serve.

CLAM   CLAM OMELETTE NORMANDE
(Clams, chives, juniper berries, Normande sauce)

Heat 1 cup drained, canned minced clams with 1 tablespoon
butter, 1 teaspoon chopped chives, a good pinch each of salt
and pepper, and 3 juniper berries, if available. Stir in ¼ cup
Normande sauce (see page 174). Make a 6-egg omelette and
before folding spread the chopped clam mixture in the center.
After folding the omelette out onto the platter, pour ¼ cup
Normande Sauce on top and serve.

CODFISH   BRANDADE OF CODFISH OMELETTE or
                         OMELETTE BÉNÉDICTINE
(Salt codfish, cream, oil, garlic, truffle, Normande Sauce)

✿ *A brandade is an unusual and delicious use of the fa-*
   miliar cod and well worth the trouble and time neces-
   sary to achieve it.

To make a brandade, soak ½ pound of salt codfish in cold water for 6 hours, changing the water once or twice. Drain, cover with fresh water, and bring to the boiling point. Poach, just below the simmer for 20 minutes. Drain and clean the fish and put through a fine meat chopper. Place the chopped fish in a mortar and work it hard with 1 tablespoon warm oil and 1 clove of chopped garlic. As it gets smooth, add, a spoonful at a time, ⅓ cup warm milk and ⅓ cup of oil, alternately. Work continually until smooth, put in the top of a double boiler, and add 1 teaspoon lemon juice, a dash each of pepper and nutmeg, and 1 tablespoon of heavy cream. The consistency should be that of mashed potato.

Place about ⅔ of a cup of brandade, to which has been added 1 small chopped truffle, in the center of a 6-egg omelette before folding out on the platter. Pour ⅓ to ½ cup Normande Sauce (see page 174) over the top and serve.

Instead of the brandade, the omelette may be filled with cooked, flaked salt codfish combined with Normande Sauce.

CRAB   PLAIN CRAB OMELETTE
(Crabmeat)

Heat 1 cup cooked flaked crabmeat in 1 heaping tablespoon of butter with a pinch each of salt and pepper and a few grains of cayenne, until the butter browns very slightly. Fold into the center of a 6- to 8-egg omelette.

CRAB   CREAMED CRAB OMELETTE
(Crabmeat, cream sauce, sherry)

✳ *There is no finer use of crabmeat than this,—and so simple, too.*

Heat 1 cup cooked, flaked crabmeat in 1 tablespoon of butter with a pinch each of salt and pepper and a few grains of cayenne. Sprinkle on and blend in ½ teaspoon of flour, add 3 tablespoons heavy cream and 1 scant tablespoon of Madeira or sherry wine. When the mixture begins to simmer, continue to cook, stirring, for 1 minute. Fold into the center of a 6- to 8-egg omelette.

CRAB   MANCHU CRAB OMELETTE
(Crabmeat, water chestnuts, mushrooms, bamboo shoots)

In a saucepan put 4 or 5 water chestnuts, ¼ cup shredded Chinese dried mushrooms, ½ cup of bamboo shoots, a little salt and pepper. Just cover with water and cook until all liquid has evaporated. Beat 8 eggs with 6 tablespoons of water and add 1 can of crabmeat, or the equivalent in fresh cooked crabmeat, and the vegetables. Make this mixture into a series of small omelettes cooked in oil on both sides, in a small pan.

FISH   LIVORNO OMELETTE
(Fish, tomato, parsley, lemon)

Cut a ¼-pound piece of any good fish of your choice into cubes, salt them lightly, and cook in 1 or 2 teaspoons of oil. When the fish is cooked mix it with 1 large tomato which has been peeled, seeded, diced, and half cooked in 1 teaspoon of oil with salt and pepper, 1 teaspoon of chopped parsley, and a little lemon juice.
Put the mixture in the center of a 6-egg omelette before folding out on the platter. (Dainty left-over bits of fish will do, of course.)

FISH   PHILIPPINE FISH OMELETTE or TORTILLA
(Fish, garlic, onion, tomato, peas)

Sauté in 2 tablespoons of lard 1 pound of fish, such as filets of haddock, flounder, cod, or other good fish of your choice.

Cook until browned on each side. Cut it in cubes. In the same fat, sauté 1 chopped clove of garlic, 1 sliced onion, 1 peeled and seeded tomato, chopped fine, and salt and pepper. Simmer for 5 minutes and add 1 teaspoon of butter, and ⅔ cup of cooked peas. Stir in the fish.

Beat 4 eggs and pour them into 1 tablespoon melted fat in the pan. When they begin to set, mix in the fish and vegetable mixture. Finish cooking and serve folded or flat, like a *frittata.*

HADDOCK   **CREAMED HADDOCK OMELETTE**
(Smoked haddock, cream)

Cover a piece of smoked haddock filet with cold water, bring slowly to a boil, cover, and let stand 15 minutes. Drain, dry, and flake off 1 cup of the fish. Sauté 2 to 3 minutes in 1 tablespoon butter, sprinkle with ½ teaspoon flour, blend, and stir in ¼ cup of cream. When hot and slightly thickened, fold into the center of a 6- to 8-egg omelette.

HADDOCK   **OMELETTE ARNOLD BENNETT**
(Smoked haddock, cream, Swiss cheese)

❀ *This recipe seems to have originated at the Savoy Grill in London and to have been named for a famous author as British as the chief ingredient.*

Soak and prepare smoked haddock as above. Beat ¾ cup of the finely flaked fish with 6 eggs when preparing the omelette. Slide the omelette out when cooked, without folding, onto a heatproof dish. Spread ½ cup of cream sauce (made with cream) over the top, sprinkle with grated Swiss cheese, and brown lightly under the broiler.

HERRING   KIPPERED HERRING OMELETTE
(Kippered herring, or other smoked fish, cream)

Cover a kippered herring with water and bring it slowly to a
boil. Drain, dry on a cloth, and cut in small pieces. Heat these
in butter, add a small amount of fresh cream, and fold into
the center of an omelette. Needless to say, left-over herring or
other smoked fish may be heated and used in this way.

LOBSTER   OMELETTE BARON DE BARANTE
(Lobster, mushrooms, Port wine, cream, Parmesan cheese)

✿ *Named for a character famous in French gastronomy,*
this was a favorite of Edward VII.
Sauté ⅓ pound sliced mushrooms in 1½ tablespoons butter
with ½ teaspoon lemon juice, salt and pepper. When softened and most of the liquid has evaporated, add 1½ tablespoons Port or Madeira wine. Cover and simmer until half
evaporated. Add ⅓ cup heavy cream and ⅓ cup sliced cooked
lobster meat. Simmer 2 minutes. Remove 3 tablespoons of
the sauce to a tiny saucepan and blend in 1 teaspoon grated
Parmesan cheese. Fold the lobster and mushroom mixture
into a 6-egg omelette, spread the extra sauce on top, sprinkle
with a little extra Parmesan, and brown lightly under a hot
broiler.

LOBSTER   OMELETTE DIEPPOISE
(Lobster, truffle, cream, lobster butter, shrimp, tomato sauce)

✿ *This is fine enough to offer any honored guest—and at*
the same time good use of luxury food in small quanti-
ties.
Heat ⅓ cup sliced, cooked lobster meat in 1 tablespoon of
butter with 1 chopped truffle, salt and pepper, and a few

grains of cayenne. Add ¼ cup heavy cream and 1 teaspoon lobster butter (see page 172). Fold into the center of a 6-egg omelette. Place a row of cooked, peeled shrimps along the top and spoon over them a small stream of fresh tomato sauce.

LOBSTER   LOBSTER OMELETTE FILIPPINI
(Lobster, white wine, cream sauce)

Heat ½ cup sliced cooked lobster meat with 1 tablespoon butter and ¼ cup dry white wine. Simmer till partly reduced and blend in ½ cup thick cream sauce (white sauce made with cream). Fold the lobster meat and part of the sauce into the center of a 6-egg omelette. Pour the rest of the sauce along the top and serve.

LOBSTER   CHINESE LOBSTER OMELETTE
(Lobster, bamboo shoots, water chestnuts, celery, mushrooms)

❀ *The Chinese are famous for their interesting combinations of flavors and textures. This mixture is no exception.*

Mix ¾ cup cooked chopped lobster meat with ¼ cup thinly sliced bamboo shoots, ¼ cup thinly sliced water chestnuts, ½ cup raw celery cut very thinly on the bias, 2 tablespoons canned mushrooms, thinly sliced, ½ teaspoon salt, ⅛ teaspoon pepper, and ½ teaspoon Chinese seasoning powder. Beat 6 eggs and mix thoroughly with the other ingredients. Make 4 individual omelettes with this mixture in a 6- to 7-inch pan, heating about 1 teaspoon of oil in the pan before pouring in each omelette. Turn them to brown lightly on both sides.

LOBSTER   OMELETTE DIPLOMATE
(Lobster, truffle, cream sauce, lobster butter, Parmesan cheese)

❀ *This is high in the scale of luxury omelettes, as distinguished as its name implies.*

This is composed of 2 round, flat omelettes, each made with 3 eggs, a lobster filling, cream sauce, and cheese on top, the whole lightly browned under the broiler. The top omelette must be quite soft, or it will dry out when the whole is being browned. Use a smaller pan when making the 2 omelettes or they will be too large and thin. Mix ¾ cup diced, cooked lobster meat and 1 large truffle, thinly sliced, and cook, stirring, over a low fire in 1 tablespoon butter for 2 minutes. Blend in half the following cream sauce reserving the rest for the top: melt 1 tablespoon butter and stir in 1 tablespoon flour. Add a pinch of pepper. Stir in very gradually 1 cup warm cream, using a sauce whisk. Simmer a few minutes until thick and add 1 tablespoon lobster butter, or about 1 teaspoon lobster paste or spread, depending on its strength of flavor. (This may be purchased in tubes or small jars.) Test for seasoning. A few drops of brandy will enhance the flavor. When your first omelette has been made and slipped out upon a round platter, place the lobster filling, mixed with half the sauce, in the center. Slide the second omelette over this, pour the remaining sauce on top, sprinkle with a little grated Swiss or Parmesan cheese, and brown quickly (1 minute or less) under a hot broiler.

LOBSTER   THE PRELATE'S OMELETTE
(Fish roe, lobster, shrimp, truffle, Normande Sauce)

❀ *This would appear to be the invention of Frédéric, French chef to a high dignitary of the church, whose re-*

*markable talents earned him the benedictions of his
master. Unfortunately he died very young, and we trust
that his "high bonnet" has taken its well deserved place
amongst the halos of the blessed.*

Slice a small carp roe in pieces and heat them in butter without allowing to boil. To this add ¼ cup of cooked diced lobster meat, 3 cooked, cleaned, and diced shrimp, and 1 teaspoon
julienne of truffle. Add ½ cup of Normande Sauce (see page
174) into which has been blended 1 teaspoon of lobster butter
(see page 172). Heat all together over a low fire without boiling and fill the omelette with this exquisite combination. Pour
a little of the same sauce over the top and sprinkle with
chopped truffle.

LOBSTER   THE CARDINAL'S OMELETTE
(Crayfish or lobster meat, Cardinal Sauce)

❁ *For this dish 10 or 12 fresh-water crayfish should be
used, the tail meat going into the dish and the remnants
being used as a base for the sauce. As this ingredient is
difficult to obtain in this country, lobster has been substituted with excellent results.*

Soak 2 tablespoons of breadcrumbs in just enough milk to
make a fairly thick paste, with salt and pepper and a dash of
nutmeg. Heat 3 tablespoons of cooked, chopped, or shredded
lobster meat in 1 tablespoon of butter and mix with the
crumbs. This constitutes your filling which is folded into the
omelette. Around the omelette is poured a small amount of
concentrated sauce which perfects this dish with its rich savor.
To make the sauce, break up a few pieces of lobster shell and
scraps, such as the small claws, and sauté them in butter together with 1 teaspoon of chopped onion, a bay leaf, and a
sprig of parsley, salt, and pepper. When browned, add 1 cup
of hot stock, cover closely, and simmer over a low fire until

the liquid is reduced to about ⅓ of its original quantity. Strain the sauce through a fine sieve, thicken if necessary with *beurre manié* (½ teaspoon of flour worked into an equal amount of butter), and pour around the omelette.

LOBSTER   JAPANESE LOBSTER OMELETTE
(Lobster, scallions, celery, stock)

Sauté about 12 finely sliced scallions and 6 tablespoons of chopped celery in 2 tablespoons of butter. When softened a little, add ¾ cup of chicken stock, 2 tablespoons of soya sauce, salt, a little paprika, ½ teaspoon of sugar, and 2 cups of diced lobster meat. Reheat and simmer 2 minutes. Beat 6 egg yolks thoroughly with 6 tablespoons of cream, salt, and pepper, and blend in the 6 whites, beaten fairly stiff. Pour the eggs into the heated butter in your omelette pan and cook as a mousseline omelette, rather slowly. When the eggs begin to cook around the edge, spread in the lobster mixture. Continue cooking and turn to brown the other side if possible. An easier method is to fold it in half and slide it out upon the platter.

MUSSEL   MUSSEL OMELETTE WITH TOMATO
                                 SAUCE
(Mussels, white wine, herbs, tomato sauce)

Put enough mussels to make ¾ cup when shelled into a covered saucepan with 2 tablespoons white wine, 1 teaspoon chopped parsley, 3 slices of onion, 1 clove of garlic, chopped, and a pinch of pepper, and steam until opened. Remove the mussels from the shells, return to the juices, and simmer 2 minutes. Drain the mussels, reserving juices, and chop coarsely. Mix with 6 eggs, beaten for an omelette. Cook and fold out. Pour on top ⅓ cup fresh tomato sauce (see page 175) into which have been blended 2 tablespoons of the mussel juices.

If preferred, fold the mussels into the center of the omelette combined with tomato sauce into which you have blended 2 tablespoons of the juices from the mussels.

MUSSEL   **MUSSEL AND SPINACH OMELETTE**
(Spinach, mussels, spices)

✤ *Here the crustaceans and the garden greens are not actually married, but friendly in their relations as is more fitting.*

Steam ½ pound of spinach in a covered pan till it renders its own juices and is cooked soft. Drain well, chop finely, return to the pan with a little salt and 1 teaspoon of butter. Heat until all moisture has evaporated.

Steam open enough mussels to make ¾ of a cup, as in foregoing recipe. Drain, keeping juices, and chop finely. Heat them in 1 teaspoon of butter, add a pinch of pepper, a pinch each of clove and cinnamon. Sprinkle with 1 teaspoon of flour and blend. Stir in ⅓ to ½ cup liquid from the mussels.

Fold the spinach into the center of a 6-egg omelette, spread the mussel sauce on top, and serve.

OYSTER   **LENTEN SEAFOOD OMELETTE**
(Oysters, shrimps, mushrooms, cream)

✤ *This combination may have been invented by a worldly churchman who considered his appetite more than his soul when avoiding meat in Lent.*

Poach one dozen fresh shelled small oysters in their juices for 2 or 3 minutes, or just until the edges begin to curl. Remove tougher outside edges, and dice them coarsely. Add 6 or 8 cooked shrimps and 3 or 4 cooked mushrooms, diced in the same way. Blend in 3 tablespoons heavy cream sauce made with equal parts of cream and the juices of the poached oysters. Add a pinch of cayenne, but no salt, heat together for 2 minutes, and test for seasoning.

Fold this filling into the center of a 6- or 8-egg omelette and serve surrounded by miniature patty shells filled with chopped truffles heated in some of the same cream sauce.

OYSTER   CREAMED OYSTER OMELETTE
(Oysters, cream)

Poach one dozen fresh shelled oysters in their juices for 2 or 3 minutes, drain them, and reserve their juices. Remove hard outside edges and slice the centers lengthwise. Melt a scant tablespoon of butter in a small saucepan, blend in the same amount of flour, and add gradually ¼ cup of the oyster liquid and ¼ cup of heavy cream. Season with a pinch of salt and a few grains of cayenne. The sauce should be quite thick, as it thins when the oysters are added. Add the oysters to this and pour into the center of a 6-egg omelette before folding, reserving a little of the sauce to spread on top.

OYSTER   OYSTER OMELETTE MOUSSELINE
(Oysters, sauce of oyster liquor and cream with celery, onion, and parsley)

Sauté in 2 tablespoons of butter 1 tablespoon each of finely chopped celery, onion, and parsley. When golden-brown, blend in 1½ tablespoons of flour, salt, and pepper, and add gradually 1½ cups of liquid composed of half top milk or thin cream and half oyster liquor. The oyster liquor is obtained as follows: heat 3 dozen smallish oysters in their own juices just until they curl. Reserve the liquid and remove the outer "beard" and hard parts of the oysters. Cut the soft centers in two lengthwise. Beat the yolks and whites of 6 eggs separately as in the directions for a mousseline omelette. Season and combine them together carefully with two thirds of the oysters. Now make your omelette in plenty of butter (according to the recipe for mousseline omelette) and when turned out on the platter, cover with the sauce to which you have added the remaining third of the oysters.

OYSTER   OMELETTE ANTOINE
(Oysters, olives, sweet peppers, tomato, parsley)

 From New Orleans comes a delightful oyster and vegetable omelette which is served flat instead of folded and constitutes a hearty main dish for lunch or Sunday night supper.

The following coarsely chopped vegetables are simmered together in a little stock until soft: 1 tablespoon of pitted green olives, 1 tablespoon of green pepper, ¼ cup canned tomato, 1 tablespoon canned or fresh sweet red pimento, and ½ tablespoon of parsley.

In another pan sauté in butter 2 tablespoons of chopped onion until soft and golden. Add this, together with 3 tablespoons of chopped oysters (the soft centers only) to the other ingredients, and simmer the whole for about 5 minutes.

Beat 6 eggs for an omelette adding a dash of Tabasco and 1 tablespoon of oil. Stir into the eggs one half the vegetable-oyster mixture and make your omelette flat like a *frittata,* cooking the top briefly under the broiler before sliding out on the platter. Surround with the remaining mixture and serve.

ROE   OMELETTE BOULONNAISE
(Fish roe, browned butter)

Brown in butter until firm a roe of mackerel or other fish. Cut it in slices and place it in the center of your omelette with 2 tablespoons of maître-d'hôtel butter made as follows:
Maître-D'Hôtel Butter—Heat the butter until it begins to brown, then add a teaspoon each of lemon juice and finely chopped parsley.

SALMON   SMOKED SALMON OMELETTE
(Smoked salmon, Bearnaise Sauce)

Place in the center of a 6-egg omelette 4 tablespoons of flaked smoked salmon over which you spread 3 or 4 tablespoons of Bearnaise Sauce (see page 171).

SALMON   CREAMED SALMON OMELETTE
(Salmon, cream sauce, parsley)

Flake ½ cup of cold, cooked salmon and heat it in ½ cup of cream sauce, adding a heaping teaspoon of finely chopped parsley. Fold into the center of a 6-egg omelette, sprinkle chopped parsley on top, and serve.

SALMON   DANISH OMELETTE
(Smoked salmon, cream sauce, capers, anchovy essence)

Cut a 2-ounce piece of smoked salmon in ¼-inch squares and drop them into boiling water. Cover, turn off heat, and let poach for 5 minutes. Drain and dry on a cloth. Mix the salmon with ½ cup of cream sauce containing ½ tablespoon of capers and keep hot.

Make a 6-egg omelette containing only a small dash of salt, a good dash of pepper, and 1 teaspoon of anchovy essence.

When folded out on the platter slit the top, spoon some of your salmon filling into this cavity and the rest along the sides of the omelette.

SCALLOPS   OMELETTE LUCULLUS
(Scallops, cheese, truffle, tongue, mushrooms, tomato sauce)

❀ *And Lucullan is the word for it!*

Cook ¾ cup of small Cape scallops in salted water until just firm. Drain and dry on a cloth. Heat them in 1 tablespoon melted butter, adding a little salt, pepper, and a pinch of nutmeg. Add 1 teaspoon of grated Parmesan cheese, 1 teaspoon chopped truffle, a generous tablespoon each of julienne of cooked tongue and raw mushrooms. Add ½ cup fresh tomato sauce and heat together without allowing the mixture to boil. Fill the center of a 6-egg omelette with this mixture, fold out, and spoon a little of the tomato sauce along the top.

SHRIMP   SHRIMP OMELETTE WITH LOBSTER
                                                    SAUCE
(Shrimp, mushrooms, cream, sherry, lobster butter)

Dice ¾ cup of peeled, cooked shrimp, first reserving a few whole ones to decorate the omelette. Slice 4 medium mushrooms and sauté in 1 teaspoon butter 3 minutes. Make a cream sauce by melting 1 tablespoon butter, blending in ¾ tablespoon flour, and stirring in gradually ¾ cup of cream.

When hot and thickened, add 1 teaspoon sherry and 1 tablespoon lobster butter (see page 172). (Or lobster paste may be
used by blending gradually a small amount of the sauce into
1 teaspoon of paste in a bowl, stirring till smooth, and return-
ing to the sauce.)
Heat all ingredients together.
Make a 6-egg omelette, fold out on the platter, and make a
slit along the top. Fill this space with the mixture, pouring
surplus along the sides of the platter. Decorate with whole
shrimps on each side and serve.

SHRIMP   SHRIMP OMELETTE MIREPOIX
(Shrimp, vegetables, herbs, tomato, white wine, brandy)

In 1½ tablespoons melted butter heat ½ carrot, grated, 1
small onion, finely chopped, ½ small stalk of celery and
leaves, finely chopped, ½ teaspoon parsley, chopped, 1 bay
leaf, a pinch each of marjoram and thyme, salt, and pepper.
Simmer for 6 to 8 minutes. Add 3 tablespoons tomato paste,
½ cup white wine, ½ cup water or light stock, 1 teaspoon
brandy. Cover and simmer for 15 to 20 minutes, or until reduced by a third. Heat 1 cup diced cooked shrimp in this
sauce and pour into the center of an 8-egg omelette, reserving
some of the sauce to pour over the top after folding out on
the platter.

SHRIMP   OMELETTE NANTUA
(Shrimp, Nantua sauce)

Mix ½ cup small cooked shrimp with ¼ cup of Nantua
sauce (see page 174) and place in the center of a 6-egg
omelette before folding out on the platter. Pour ¼ cup of the
sauce along the top.

SHRIMP   OMELETTE VANDERBILT
(Shrimp, green pepper, tomato, Madeira sauce)

Skin 1 green pepper by first heating on all sides in hot oil and
then allowing to cool enough to handle. Empty it of seeds
and cut in very thin slivers. Put them in a saucepan with 1
peeled sliced tomato, 6 cooked cleaned shrimps cut in pieces,
and 1 or 2 tablespoons of Madeira sauce (see page 173). Season with salt and pepper and simmer for about 15 minutes.
Make a 6-egg omelette and fill it with the thicker part of your
shrimp mixture lifted out with a draining spoon. Pour around
the omelette the remaining sauce (boiled down a little to reduce it if necessary.)

SHRIMP   WALDORF SHRIMP OMELETTE
(Shrimps, green pepper, sauce, lobster butter)

Make 1 cup of sauce by blending 1 tablespoon of butter with
1 tablespoon of flour and stirring in gradually 1 cup of good
chicken or veal stock. Add 1 teaspoon of lobster butter (see
page 172) and 12 cooked and cleaned shrimps. Cook for 3
minutes, stirring slightly. Add about ¼ of a green pepper,
finely chopped, and simmer for 10 minutes longer. Use half of
this mixture to fill a 6-egg omelette and pour the rest along
the sides after folding out on the platter.

SHRIMP   CHINESE SHRIMP AND VEGETABLE
                                          OMELETTE
(Mushrooms, bamboo shoots, shrimps, onion)

❀ *This is an adaptation of a Chinese dish whose ingredients
   may all be purchased in this country. It should make 6
   servings.*
Wash 4 dried mushrooms and soak them in a little water for
½ hour. Or you may use ½ cup cooked fresh or canned

mushrooms. Remove their stems and cut them in thin slices. Add to them ½ cup sliced bamboo shoots, ¾ cup cooked cleaned shrimps cut in small pieces, and 1 tablespoon of soya sauce. Fry this mixture in 1 tablespoon of hot oil for 3 minutes.

Beat 4 eggs for an omelette and add to them ¼ cup finely chopped spring onions (scallions) with part of the green tops, 1½ teaspoons soya, a pinch of salt, and 3 tablespoons of water.

Make tiny omelettes in your smallest pan using about 3 tablespoons of the egg mixture for each. Heat a small amount of oil in the pan before making each omelette. As each omelette browns a little on the bottom, fill it with 1 tablespoon of the shrimp mixture and fold it up. Serve side by side on a warm platter.

SHRIMP   CHINESE SHRIMP OMELETTE (Eggs Foo
                                                    Yung)
(Shrimp, pork, onions, bean sprouts)

Beat 4 eggs and mix them with ½ cup of cooked, diced shrimp, ½ cup finely chopped onions, ¼ cup chopped roast pork, 2 cups of bean sprouts, salt, and pepper.
Of this mixture make 3 separate flat omelettes, cooked in a little oil, browned on both sides. Serve with Chinese sauce (see page 171).

TUNAFISH   TUNAFISH OMELETTE WITH
                              ANCHOVY BUTTER
(Tunafish, anchovy butter)

Add ¼ cup of diced canned tunafish, drained of its oil, to 6 eggs beaten for an omelette. Cook the omelette in the usual way and when folded out on the platter, pour 2 tablespoons of melted anchovy butter (see page 171) along the top.

TUNAFISH   ITALIAN TUNA OMELETTE
(Tunafish, herbs, anchovy)

For a 4-egg omelette, or *frittata,* rub the bowl with garlic before breaking in the eggs. Beat them lightly and add a small pinch of salt, a larger pinch of pepper, 1 teaspoon chopped parsley, ½ teaspoon orégano or marjoram, 2 chopped anchovy filets, and a small can of grated tunafish. Cook this omelette slowly in 2 tablespoons of olive oil instead of butter, about 6 minutes on each side, adding more oil to the pan before cooking the second side. Serve flat on a round platter.

TUNAFISH   OMELETTE DU CURÉ OF
                                     BRILLAT-SAVARIN
(Tunafish, fish roe, shallot, onion)

❀ *The story of this omelette is world famous, it having
   originated with the cook of Madame Récamier's curé.
   But its beauty is undimmed by time.*
Take one fresh carp, herring, or mackerel roe and parboil it for 5 minutes in simmering salted water. If the roe is large, use only half of it. Drain, cool, and cut into dice. Dice also in bits about 2 tablespoons drained, white tunafish. Add salt and pepper, 1 small shallot, chopped, or 1 teaspoon chopped onion. Put all into a heated saucepan with 2 tablespoons sweet butter. Now they must steep together over a very low fire until the butter is well melted and the mixture blended. Handle as lightly and as little as possible to avoid breaking

up the roe. Under no circumstances allow the mixture to boil or brown. Blend this gently with 8 beaten and seasoned eggs and cook your omelette. In a small saucepan melt 1 tablespoon sweet butter together with a scant teaspoon of lemon juice, a pinch each of salt and pepper, and 1 teaspoon finely chopped parsley. Heat together for 2 or 3 minutes and pour this maître d'hôtel sauce into the center of a warm omelette platter. Upon this turn out your folded omelette, still soft and delicately cooked, and serve at once.

TUNAFISH   OMELETTE FRÉDÉRIC
(Tunafish, fish roe, shallot, meat extract, tomato paste, lobster butter)

❀ *The legendary Frédéric here improved upon the curé's omelette. More complicated, but worth the trouble.*
This is a variation of Brillat-Savarin's recipe.
Plunge 1 carp, haddock, or mackerel roe into simmering salted water for 5 minutes. If a large roe, use half of it. Slice it in half-inch slices and dice them. Sauté in 1 tablespoon butter turning very carefully. In another small pan sauté 3 tablespoons diced white tunafish, drained and wiped. Season both lightly with salt and pepper. Sauté ½ a small shallot, chopped, in 1 teaspoon butter for 2 minutes, add 1 small teaspoon of *glace de viande* or condensed meat extract, 1 teaspoon tomato paste, ¼ cup water, and 2 teaspoons lobster butter (see page 172). When blended, stir in ⅓ cup of cream, a pinch of cayenne and salt. Add the roe and tuna to the sauce at the last minute to avoid breaking up the roe. Pour some of this filling into a 6-egg omelette before folding and place the rest on each side of the platter.

WHITEBAIT   RUSSIAN WHITEBAIT OMELETTE
(Whitebait, sour cream)

Clean and bone ¾ cup of whitebait or minnows and fry them
carefully in butter until golden.
Beat 6 eggs for an omelette and add to them 2 tablespoons of
sour cream, salt and pepper, and ½ tablespoon of chopped
fresh fennel or dill. Pour them over the fish, stir all together,
and allow to set. Fold over once and turn out on the platter.
Serve sour cream with this omelette.

WHITEBAIT   WHITEBAIT FRITTATA
(Whitebait, parsley)

Clean and wash ½ pound of whitebait and dry them on a
cloth. Sprinkle with salt and pepper and 1 teaspoon finely
chopped parsley. Beat and season 6 eggs for an omelette and
stir in the fish. Heat 4 tablespoons of butter in your omelette
pan, pour in the mixture, and stir a little to distribute evenly.
Allow to brown on the bottom and turn, if you can, to brown
the other side. Or if you prefer, finish cooking under the
broiler with a little melted butter poured on top. The trick is
to cook it just enough without drying out the eggs.

POULTRY AND GAME
OMELETTES

POULTRY AND GAME
OMELETTES

All of the many types of poultry and game which exist have not been mentioned separately in these recipes, as substitutions are obvious. Pheasant, guinea fowl, ducks—wild or domestic—furred or feathered game of any sort may be used to make palatable omelettes. Turkey meat in place of chicken goes almost without saying. One turkey liver may take the place of several chicken livers, and mushrooms substituted for truffles when necessary.

CHICKEN (OR TURKEY) OMELETTE À LA BRETONNE
(Chicken, leek, celery, cream sauce)

Slice into fine strips (julienne) 1 leek and 1 stalk of celery and sauté in 1 tablespoon of butter until soft but not brown. Make a purée of chicken by putting ½ cup of cooked chicken through the finest blade of a meat grinder and combining it with 1 teaspoon of melted butter blended with 1 teaspoon of flour and 3 tablespoons of cream, salt, and pepper. Combine the purée and vegetables and fill a 6-egg omelette with this mixture. Pour 3 or 4 tablespoons of cream sauce or Normande sauce (see page 174) over the top before serving.

CHICKEN   OMELETTE NANTUA
(Chicken, truffle, Nantua sauce)

Heat ¾ cup of diced cooked chicken meat with ½ truffle,
sliced, in 1 tablespoon of butter. Add 2 or 3 tablespoons of
hot chicken stock, reheat, and fill a 6-egg omelette with this
mixture before folding, and pour over the top ½ cup of
Nantua sauce (see page 174).

CHICKEN   OMELETTE ALBINA
(Chicken, onion, truffle, stock)

Sauté ½ an onion, finely chopped, in 1 tablespoon butter
until soft. Add 1 small truffle, sliced, salt, and pepper and
simmer 1 minute. Heat ½ cup juices from a roast chicken,
(or melt ½ teaspoon beef extract in ½ cup hot chicken
stock), and blend this into 1 teaspoon potato starch. Return
to the pan and simmer until thickened. Combine about ½ of
this liquid with the onion, truffle, and ½ cup finely minced
cooked chicken. Simmer for 1 minute and fill a 6-egg omelette
with this fine chicken hash. Add 3 tablespoons of cream to
the rest of the sauce and pour it along each side of the omelette on the platter.

CHICKEN   OMELETTE MAINTENON
(Chicken, mushrooms, truffle, sherry, cream sauce)

❀   *Madame de Maintenon was known as a strict "gover-
     ness" in the household of Louis XIV. Perhaps she al-
     lowed him this delicacy as an occasional treat.*
Sauté 3 mushrooms, sliced, in 1 tablespoon butter until softened, add 1 large truffle, finely diced, and ½ cup cooked,

diced, white meat of chicken, salt, and pepper. Sprinkle on 1 teaspoon of potato starch and blend well. Now add gradually ¼ cup warmed chicken stock and 1 tablespoon heavy cream. Simmer together for 1 to 2 minutes and add 1 teaspoon of sherry.

Make a cream sauce with 1 tablespoon butter, ½ tablespoon flour, salt and pepper, and ½ to ¾ cup of light cream. Slice 1 large onion and cook it down slowly in butter until soft but not brown. Mash through a sieve and add to the cream sauce. Put the chicken mixture in the center of a 6-egg omelette before folding, pour the cream-onion sauce over the top, sprinkle with a little grated Parmesan cheese and melted butter, and brown lightly under the broiler.

CHICKEN   OMELETTE AGNÈS SOREL
(Chicken, mushrooms, ham or tongue, meat juices)

❀ *This omelette is named for another famous lady in French history, perhaps indicating she had good taste in cookery as well as other gifts.*

Make a chicken hash as for Omelette Albina (see page 54), substituting 2 or 3 mushrooms, sliced and sautéed, for the truffle. Fill a 6-egg omelette with this mixture and when folded out on the platter sprinkle along the top 2 or 3 tablespoons of finely shredded boiled tongue or ham. On this pour 2 or 3 tablespoons of concentrated veal stock, or a sauce made of ½ teaspoon meat concentrate and a lump of butter melted in 3 tablespoons of hot stock.

CHICKEN   OMELETTE IMPERATRICE
(Chicken, oysters, mushrooms)

Sauté in butter 2 sliced mushrooms. Add the soft centers of 6 fresh oysters, a little of their liquor, and 3 tablespoons of

cooked chicken meat cut in thin julienne strips. Season with
salt and pepper, and when the oysters are just cooked but still
soft, cut them in half lengthwise. Fill a 6-egg omelette with
this mixture and pour over the top a little sauce made with
hot chicken stock slightly thickened with 1 teaspoon of butter
and 1 teaspoon of flour worked thoroughly together.

CHICKEN LIVER   OMELETTE FOIES DE VOLAILLES
(Chicken liver, tomato sauce)

❀   *The next time you roast a chicken, save the liver to make
    this omelette the next day.*
For a 4-egg omelette sauté 1 good sized chicken liver lightly
in butter for 2 or 3 minutes, or until cooked but slightly pink
in the center. Chop coarsely and fold into the center of the
omelette. Pour along the top a few spoonfuls of tomato
sauce made by combining 1 tablespoon tomato paste and ½
teaspoon of butter with a little meat stock to thin to desired
consistency. Sprinkle with finely chopped parsley and serve.

CHICKEN LIVER   OMELETTE CHASSEUR
(Chicken livers, mushrooms, shallot, white wine)

❀   *This is a classic French omelette as taught at a famous
    cooking school in Paris.*
For a 6-egg omelette use 2 chicken livers and 2 or 3 mushrooms. Cut each chicken liver in 4 to 6 pieces and sauté them
in 1 tablespoon butter with a dash of salt and pepper and ⅓
teaspoon finely chopped shallot (or onion) for barely 30 to
40 seconds. Take care not to burn the shallot or overcook the
chicken livers lest they become hard. Sprinkle with ⅓ teaspoon of flour, blend, add 1 tablespoon dry white wine, 1

tablespoon stock or water, and the mushrooms, thinly sliced and previously cooked in a little butter 4 to 5 minutes. Now make your omelette, fold it out carefully on the platter, and make a slit along the top surface without cutting through the bottom or the ends. Fill the cut with the chicken-liver mixture, sprinkle with finely chopped parsley, and serve.

CHICKEN LIVER   TURKISH OMELETTE
(Chicken liver, rice, curry)

Fry ½ cup of left-over fluffy rice in butter until it has taken on a little color. Moisten with 3 tablespoons of chicken stock and stir in 1 cooked chicken liver which has been mashed to a purée and ½ teaspoon of curry powder. Simmer together briefly and fill a 6-egg omelette with this mixture.

CHICKEN LIVER   OMELETTE FINANCIÈRE
(Chicken livers, olives, mushrooms, truffle, pickles)

❀ *This unusual combination of flavors blends into something quite exquisite, proving that the whole is greater than the sum of its parts.*
Cut 2 raw chicken livers in 3 or 4 pieces each and sauté for 1 minute in 1 tablespoon of melted butter on a moderate heat. Add 2 tablespoons of sherry, ¾ teaspoon of meat extract, 6 tablespoons water, 4 pitted sliced olives, 4 small canned mushrooms (or 3 fresh ones, sliced and precooked in butter), 1 sliced truffle, 1 or 2 small sour pickles, sliced, ½ teaspoon finely chopped parsley, salt and pepper, and a dash of cayenne. Stir, reheat, and cook for 2 minutes. If there is not enough sauce, add a little hot water.
Pour this mixture into the center of a 6-egg omelette before folding out on the platter.

CHICKEN LIVER   CHICKEN LIVER AND TOMATO
                                           OMELETTE
(Chicken livers, tomato sauce)

Cut 3 chicken livers in 4 pieces each and sauté them in 1 tablespoon hot melted butter for 1 minute. Season with salt and a dash of cayenne, add 1 tablespoon of sherry, 1½ tablespoons of tomato sauce, ½ teaspoon of meat extract, cook for 3 to 4 minutes, and fold into the center of a 6-egg omelette.

CHICKEN LIVER   OMELETTE À LA DIABLE
(Chicken livers, bacon, herbs, cheese, cream)

Melt but do not brown 1 tablespoon of butter and add salt and pepper, 1 teaspoon of chopped parsley, ½ teaspoon of chopped chervil, ½ teaspoon of chopped chives or young green onion tops, 1 clove of garlic, chopped. Steep a minute or two in the hot butter and add 3 chicken livers cut in pieces, 1 tablespoon of diced bacon. Increase the heat, stir, and allow to brown slightly. Add ½ tablespoon of grated Swiss or Parmesan cheese. Stir in 1 to 2 tablespoons of heavy cream. Fold this preparation into the center of a 6-egg omelette, sprinkle grated cheese on top, and brown lightly under the broiler.

CHICKEN AND VEGETABLE   VIENNESE CHICKEN AND
                                  VEGETABLE OMELETTE
(Chicken, peas, string beans, cauliflower, mushrooms)

❀ *This recipe makes excellent use of bits of leftovers—*
   vegetables, chicken, or giblets—though there is nothing

to hinder you from starting anew with fresh ingredients if you prefer.

Blend 2 tablespoons of flour into 2 tablespoons of melted butter and add gradually 1 cup of vegetable stock saved from the cooking of your vegetables. Cook, stirring until thick. To this add 2 tablespoons of cooked peas, 2 tablespoons of diced cooked string beans, and ¾ cup of cooked cauliflower in pieces. Sauté 3 or 4 sliced mushrooms in butter and add them to the first ingredients, together with ¾ cup diced, cooked chicken or giblets. Beat 1 egg yolk in 3 tablespoons of cream and add this to the combination, heating and stirring briefly. Make 3 plain omelettes of 3 eggs each and place ⅓ of the filling in the center of each. Fold and serve.

COCKS' COMBS AND KIDNEYS   OMELETTE À LA
                                                         ROYALE

(Cocks' combs and kidneys, truffles, foie gras, sauce of cream, meat juice, and Port wine.)

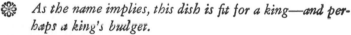 *As the name implies, this dish is fit for a king—and perhaps a king's budget.*

Sauté 3 mushrooms, sliced, in 1 tablespoon butter and add to them 1 truffle, sliced, and ½ cup of cocks' combs and kidneys. When heated together, sprinkle on a pinch of potato starch (about ½ teaspoon), add 1 teaspoon of meat glaze or beef extract, and 4 to 5 tablespoons of heavy cream. Make a small omelette of 3 to 4 eggs, mixed with 2 tablespoons of finely chopped truffle parings, and fill it with the mixture before folding.

Now make a larger omelette of 5 to 6 eggs rather thinly spread in a large pan and fold the first omelette within it.

Place on a long oval platter and along the surface put a row of small slices of foie gras with a slice of truffle between each.

Surround by a ring of sauce made with 1 tablespoon butter blended with 1 scant tablespoon flour, 2 tablespoons meat extract or strong stock, ½ to ⅔ cup of cream, and 1 tablespoon of Port wine.

DUCK LIVER   ROUEN OMELETTE
(Duck liver, meat juices, red wine)

❀ *The next time you roast a duck keep the liver and a little of the juices from the duck to make the following simple omelette.*
Cook a duck's liver in butter until done but not hard and mash it to a purée. Fold it into the center of an omelette and pour over it a little sauce made of 2 tablespoons of the brown juices left from a roast duck and 2 tablespoons of red wine simmered together for a minute.

FOIE GRAS   OMELETTE À LA BIGOURDANE
(Foie gras, truffles, Madeira sauce)

Fill a 4-egg omelette with several tablespoons of diced foie gras, or purée of foie gras, mixed with 1 or 2 truffles, sliced and warmed in butter. Spread along the surface a little Madeira or Perigord sauce (see page 174) before serving.

FOIE GRAS   OMELETTE WITH FAT OF FOIE GRAS
(Fat of foie gras, spices)

Use the fat that surrounds a pâté of foie gras—or any other good pâté for that matter—to cook this omelette. Season the eggs when beating them with salt and pepper and a pinch each of cinnamon, clove, nutmeg, and ginger. Cook the omelette in fat of foie gras. If a few particles of the meat of the pâté are involved, so much the better.

GAME   OMELETTE À LA SAINT-HUBERT
(Livers of game birds and wild rabbit, onions, mushrooms, truffles, Madeira wine)

✤ *This omelette is fittingly named for the patron saint of the hunt.*

Sauté in butter 1 small onion, chopped, until soft and pale-gold in color. Remove and in the saucepan sauté 2 mushrooms, sliced, for 2 or 3 minutes. These are mixed with the 6 eggs for your omelette, together with salt and pepper, before cooking.

For the filling brown quickly in butter several livers of pheasant, partridge, or other game birds, leaving them very rare. Remove and keep hot. In the same butter (fat of game birds is even better) cook quickly and briefly the sliced liver of a wild hare or rabbit. Add this to the birds' livers. Now heat for a few seconds 1 or 2 truffles, sliced, in the same pan. With these ingredients put sliced gizzards of your game birds previously boiled in stock. These delicacies are all mingled together with a little Madeira sauce (see page 173) to fill your omelette. When folded out on the platter, spread a thread of browned butter along the top and serve.

GAME   OMELETTE DIANA
(Cold roast wild game birds, truffles)

✤ *Diana the huntress lends her name to this game omelette.*

Mix 3 sliced, sautéed mushrooms with the eggs before making a 6-egg omelette. Make the filling of leftover roast partridge, pheasant, wild duck, or other game bird, diced and heated with a little of the juices or sauce of the roast. Place a row of sliced truffles on top and spread a thread of the sauce on these before serving.

GAME   COLD GAME OMELETTES
(Cold roast game birds, ham, stock)

For the traveler or for picnics, prepare a number of small 1-egg omelettes in a tiny pan, cooking them lightly on both sides. Leave them spread flat side by side on a baking sheet to cool.

Put ¼ pound of cooked pheasant, partridge, or wild duck meat through a meat grinder, add a pinch of cayenne, 1 tablespoon sweet butter, and 2 or 3 tablespoons cold stock made from the carcasses of the birds or juices of the roast, which should be reduced to a thick consistency or previously thickened with a little potato starch. Work in a mortar together with 2 tablespoons of finely ground chopped ham until you obtain a smooth thick purée. Spread a thin layer on each little individual omelette, roll them up, wrap separately in wax paper, and chill in the refrigerator.

VENISON   VIENNESE GAME OMELETTE
(Venison, parsley, mushrooms)

Put enough cooked venison through the meat grinder to make 1 cup. To this add 4 chopped and sautéed mushrooms, 1 tablespoon finely chopped parsley, 1 egg yolk, 1 tablespoon melted butter, a pinch each of salt and pepper. Reheat until well blended and fold into the center of a 6-egg omelette. Serve with Madeira sauce (see page 173).

VENISON, LIVER OF   **VENISON LIVER OMELETTE**
(Venison liver, herbs)

Parboil a small venison liver in salted water with parsley, 1
bay leaf, thyme, pepper, and several cloves. Drain and allow
to cool. Take the desired amount for a 6-egg omelette (about
1 cup) and mash it to a purée in a mortar. Mix this with the
seasoned eggs beaten for an omelette and make it in the
usual way.

WILD HARE OR RABBIT, LIVER OF   **HUNTERS'**
OMELETTE
(Liver of wild hare, bacon, herbs)

Chop the liver of a wild hare and scrape it with the blade of
the knife to make a purée, removing all fibers. Chop finely 1
tablespoon of bacon, 1 teaspoon of parsley, and 1 shallot.
Season all with salt, pepper, a good pinch of nutmeg and beat
these ingredients in with 6 eggs. Make of this two thin omelettes, rather thoroughly cooked, and serve them flat on a
round platter.

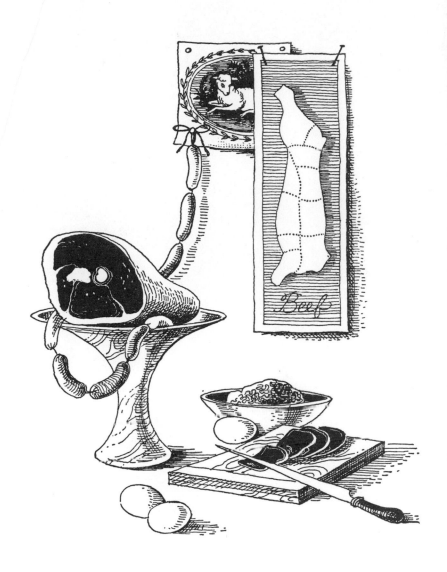

MEAT OMELETTES

MEAT OMELETTES

BACON   OMELETTE BONNE FEMME (1)
(Bacon, onion, mushrooms)

❀ *The good woman who invented this one did us all a service.*

Sauté ¾ cup diced bacon until lightly browned. Remove the pieces from the pan and sauté 1 onion, sliced, in the fat until golden and soft. When the onion is almost cooked, add 2 mushrooms, sliced, and cook about 2 minutes longer. Drain off any excess fat. Beat up 6 eggs for your omelette and stir in these ingredients just before pouring the eggs into the pan. Fold out and serve.

BACON   OMELETTE BONNE FEMME (2)
(Bacon, potato, bread croutons, herbs, tomato sauce)

❀ *Here she decided to gild the lily, but to good effect.*

Sauté 4 tablespoons of bacon cubes in a frying pan until moderately brown. Remove and in the fat sauté slowly 2 tablespoons diced, boiled potato. When these are brown on all sides, remove them in turn and sauté slowly 2 tablespoons diced bread or crusts. When these ingredients are all done to crisp golden perfection, add them to 6 eggs, beaten for an omelette, together with the salt and pepper, 1 teaspoon finely chopped parsley, and ½ teaspoon chopped chives.

Make the omelette in the usual way, fold out and serve with 2 or 3 tablespoons of tomato sauce poured along the sides.

BACON   OMELETTE BRAVAUDE
(Bacon, potato, cream, cheese)

Brown ¾ cup of bacon cubes, drain, and brown ½ cup of
diced cooked potatoes in the fat after the bacon has been removed. Add these to 6 beaten eggs prepared for an omelette.
When the omelette is just ready to fold out, pour 2 tablespoons of heavy cream in the center, sprinkle with 1 tablespoon grated Swiss cheese, fold, and serve.

BACON   OMELETTE LORRAINE (1)
(Bacon, cream, cheese)

❊   *Lorraine is famous for smoking the pig in various forms.
Bacon is the basis for these Lorraine omelettes.*
Broil 6 slices of bacon moderately on each side, keeping them
as flat as possible. Remove and drain on paper.
Beat 6 eggs for your omelette with 2 tablespoons of heavy
cream, 2 tablespoons of Swiss cheese cut in extremely thin
chips on the coarse grater, salt, and pepper. When the butter
is hot in your omelette pan, add a spoonful of the bacon fat,
pour in the eggs, and place immediately the 6 bacon strips
side by side so that they will be imbedded in the eggs as they
cook. Cook this omelette moderately firm but still creamy, do
not fold, but slide bacon-side-up onto a round dish.

BACON   OMELETTE LORRAINE (2)
(Bacon, chives, cheese)

For a 6-egg omelette add to the eggs before pouring into the
pan 4 tablespoons diced bacon, sautéed slowly until brown, 1

teaspoon chopped chives, 2 tablespoons Swiss cheese, coarsely
grated, salt, and pepper. This omelette may be served flat or
folded.

BACON   BACON OMELETTE SUZANNE
(Bacon, herbs, meat juice)

Add 4 tablespoons crisply browned diced bacon to the beaten
eggs for a 6-egg omelette, together with 1 tablespoon finely
chopped parsley and 1 teaspoon chopped chives. When the
omelette is folded out on the platter, pour 2 tablespoons of
concentrated meat juice or gravy along the surface.

BACON   OMELETTE PAYSANNE (1)
(Bacon, herbs, sorrel)

Brown 4 tablespoons diced bacon and drain on paper. In the
fat sauté gently 2 or 3 scallions or young spring onions, cut in
½-inch pieces including part of the green stems. To these ingredients add 2 tablespoons chopped, cooked sorrel, ½ clove
of garlic, chopped and mashed, and 1 teaspoon chopped
parsley. Mix all ingredients into the eggs before making the
omelette.

BACON   OMELETTE PAYSANNE (2)
(Bacon, herbs, sorrel, potatoes)

This is the same as Omelette Paysanne (1), except that ¾
cup of diced, cooked potatoes are browned and added to the
other ingredients, and the omelette is left flat, cooked a little
on each side, like a *frittata*.

BACON   PIORA OMELETTE
(Bacon, cheese, mustard)

Add 1 to 2 tablespoons of finely diced Swiss cheese and 1
teaspoon of French mustard to the other seasonings when
beating up 6 eggs for an omelette.
Sauté 2 tablespoons of diced lean bacon in 1 tablespoon of
butter in the frying pan until slightly browned, pour in the
eggs, stir all together, and allow the eggs to set before folding
out on the platter.

BACON   COLD SAVOY OMELETTE
(Bacon, chives)

Melt 1 tablespoon of butter in the frying pan and drop in 2
to 3 tablespoons of diced lean bacon and 1 tablespoon of
chopped chives. When the bacon begins to brown, drop in 6
eggs beaten for an omelette. Stir. When done on one side,
turn and cook a little on the other. A large pan should be
used as the omelette should be thin as a pancake. Or if you
prefer, make several thin omelettes in a small pan. Roll the
omelettes up, allow to cool, and wrap in waxed paper. This
is a satisfying picnic dish for the traveler or huntsman.

BACON   CHAMBÉRY OMELETTE
(Bacon, leeks, potatoes, cheese)

In 1 tablespoon of butter sauté 1 tablespoon of diced bacon,
1 finely sliced leek, and 2 tablespoons boiled, diced potato.
When browned, fill the center of a 6-egg omelette with this

mixture. Fold it out, sprinkle with grated Swiss cheese, and glaze under a hot broiler.

BACON   GERMAN OMELETTE WITH BACON
(Bacon, chives)

Broil 4 slices of bacon on both sides until crisp. Drain on paper. Crumble them into bits and add them to the batter for German omelette together with a generous teaspoon of chopped chives. Make 2 thin omelettes in the usual way (see page 22), roll up, and cut in sections.

BEEF   OMELETTE À LA MÉNAGÈRE
(Beef, onion, parsley)

Sauté in 1 tablespoon of butter 1 rather large, sliced onion until soft. Add 3 to 4 tablespoons leftover boiled or roast beef, diced, and 1 teaspoon of chopped parsley. Mix into the eggs before making the omelette. Serve flat on a round plate.

BEEF   OMELETTE RASPAIL
(Beef, bacon, ham, onion, mushrooms)

Sauté 2 tablespoons diced bacon, remove and drain on paper. Add a little butter to the remaining fat if necessary and sauté briefly 1 small onion, chopped, and 2 mushrooms, chopped. To this add 2 tablespoons minced leftover roast beef, 2 tablespoons diced ham, and 1 teaspoon chopped parsley. Heat all ingredients together and spread them in the center of a 6-egg omelette before folding. A little tomato sauce over the top of of the omelette is the finishing touch.

BEEF   SMOKED BEEF OMELETTE (1)
(Smoked beef)

Cut up finely ¾ cup smoked beef and sauté lightly in 1
tablespoon butter. Mix with 6 eggs before making the omelette.

BEEF   SMOKED BEEF OMELETTE (2)
(Smoked beef, cream)

Cook smoked beef as above and add 3 tablespoons heavy
cream before folding into the center of the omelette.

BEEF   OMELETTE VIVEUR
(Beef, artichoke, celeriac)

Dice the base of 1 cooked aritchoke and sauté it in 1 tablespoon of butter. Remove the artichoke and in the same pan
sauté 2 tablespoons of diced, cooked celeriac (celery root).
Remove this in turn and brown very quickly and briefly ⅛ of
a pound of raw, diced tenderloin of beef, seasoning it with
salt and pepper.
Beat 6 eggs with salt and pepper and a little chopped chervil
and parsley, stir in the other ingredients, and make the omelette, serving it flat on a round platter.

BRAINS   OMELETTE À LA CERVELLE
(Brains, cream, tomato sauce, mushrooms, Madeira wine)

Clean and parboil a calves' or sheeps' brain. When cooked,
mash to a soft consistency on the fire. To ¾ cupful of brains

add 3 tablespoons of cream, salt, and pepper. Spread this on the omelette before it is quite done. Fold out and pour over the top ½ cup of tomato sauce containing 2 sliced sautéed mushrooms and 1 teaspoon of Madeira wine.

BRAINS   OMELETTE WITH FRIED BRAINS
(Brains, brown butter, and vinegar)

Soak a small calves' brain in cold water for half an hour, clean, and remove all hard sinews. Place it in a saucepan with salt, 2 tablespoons of vinegar, a bay leaf, and enough cold water to cover. Bring to a boil and boil for 8 minutes. Drain and dry it and cut it in slices. These are rolled lightly in flour, shaking off all excess, and then fried delicately in butter about 3 minutes on each side. A 6-egg omelette is folded out on a platter, and the fried slices of brains arranged around it. Melt 2 tablespoons of butter in the pan in which the brains were fried, allow it to brown a little, stir in 1 teaspoon of tarragon vinegar, and pour it over the slices of fried brains.

HAM   SIMPLE HAM OMELETTE
(Ham)

For a 6-egg omelette mix 3 tablespoons of ground lean ham with the beaten eggs just before cooking. Fold out the omelette while the center is still soft. Since ham is salty, add less salt than usual to the eggs.

HAM   CREAMED HAM OMELETTE
(Ham, cream sauce)

Heat 3 tablespoons ground ham in 1 tablespoon butter, sprinkle with 1 scant teaspoon of flour, a pinch of nutmeg, and a pinch of pepper. Blend in 3 to 4 tablespoons of cream. When hot and slightly thickened, spread this mixture in the center of a 4- to 6-egg omelette before folding.

HAM   COLD HAM OMELETTE
(Ham, chicken, mustard)

❀   *An interesting substitute for picnic sandwiches is the cold ham omelette.*

Make a 4-egg omelette in a pan large enough to spread the eggs rather thinly. Place under the broiler just long enough to dry the top. When cooked, slide it whole and flat onto a plate to cool. Work in a mortar enough finely chopped ham and chopped cooked chicken, in equal quantities, to cover the surface of your omelette. Add to this enough cold butter to make your meat cling together. Season with salt, pepper, and a little powdered mustard. Spread this purée on the omelette, roll it up, wrap in wax paper, and chill in the refrigerator.

If you prefer, make a number of small omelettes with 3 good tablespoons of beaten egg to each one. Four eggs makes 8 small omelettes. Cook on both sides lightly and cool before spreading on the filling.

HAM   OMELETTE LANDAISE
(Ham, bread)

Fry in oil, or other fat, thin slices of French bread until gold and crisp. Place them in the bottom of a shallow oven dish and pour over them 4 beaten eggs combined with ½ to ¾ cup of diced ham. Cook this omelette in the oven until just done, without allowing it to dry out. Serve in the dish in which it has been cooked.

HAM   OMELETTE BÉARNAISE
(Ham, onion, pimento, tomato, parsley)

❀ *Ingredients native to the province of Béarn distinguish
  this omelette.*
Sauté in goose fat, or other good fat, 1 onion, chopped, and 1
sweet pimento, chopped. When partly done, add ⅓ to ½ cup
diced ham and 1 large tomato, peeled, emptied of its seeds,
and coarsely chopped. Simmer all together 3 to 4 minutes
and fold this mixture into the center of an omelette made of
4 to 6 eggs beaten up with 1 tablespoon of chopped parsley.

HAM   OMELETTE BAYONNAISE
(Ham, mushrooms, Béarnaise sauce, bread croutons)

❀ *Bayonne is famous for its fine smoked hams.*
Sauté in butter ½ cup of diced ham and 2 or 3 mushrooms,
diced. Combine with a generous tablespoon of Béarnaise
sauce (see page 171) just before placing the mixture in the
center of your omelette. Fold out on the platter and serve
surrounded by bread croutons fried in butter.

HAM   OMELETTE ALPHONSE XIII
(Ham, cream, ginger)

Sauté briefly ¾ cup diced ham in 1 tablespoon butter. Sprinkle on ½ teaspoon flour, blend, and stir in ¼ cup of cream.
Add a pinch of pepper, simmer, and stir until slightly thickened. Make a 6-egg omelette and fold it out on a platter.
Make a careful slit in the top, fill with the ham mixture, and

sprinkle powdered ginger on the top. Delicious and very individual!

HAM   OMELETTE BOHÉMIENNE
(Ham, truffle, parsley)

One-half cup of fine julienne of ham, 1 truffle also cut into fine julienne strips, and 1 tablespoon chopped parsley are stirred into the 6 beaten eggs before making this omelette. A trickle of brown butter along the top after folding on the platter is the finishing touch.

HAM   OMELETTE BROUILLÉE or SCRAMBLED
                                               OMELETTE
(Ham, truffle, mushrooms, Mornay sauce, cheese, bread croutons, tomato purée)

Cut 2 truffles into fine julienne, with an equal quantity of julienne of ham or tongue and the same amount of cooked sliced mushrooms. Beat 6 eggs for an omelette, adding a pinch of cayenne pepper with the other seasonings. Melt a generous tablespoon of butter in your pan and when hot, pour in the eggs, stirring with a large fork until they begin to take on a certain consistency. Now mix in quickly the other ingredients, together with 1 teaspoon of butter, and remove the mixture to a cold oval-shaped oven dish before the eggs become too dry and hard. Shape this with a knife or spatula into the form of an omelette and pour over the top a layer of Mornay sauce (½ to ¾ cup) (see page 173). Sprinkle grated Parmesan cheese on the top and brown quickly and briefly under a hot broiler. Surround the omelette with round fried bread croutons, placing a spoonful of tomato purée on each crouton. A fitting dish for any king!

HAM   OMELETTE À LA FERMIÈRE
(Ham, vegetables)

Parboil 2 tablespoons diced carrots for 2 minutes, drain, and sauté in butter with 1 tablespoon coarsely chopped onion and 2 tablespoons diced celery. When the whole is soft, season with salt and pepper and add 1 tablespoon chopped parsley. Add the vegetables to 6 beaten eggs for your omelette.
Heat 2 tablespoons diced ham in 1 tablespoon hot butter in the omelette pan, pour the eggs with the vegetable mixture over the ham, and cook until firm but not dry. Do not fold, but serve flat on a round platter.

HAM   OMELETTE À LA GASCONNE
(Ham, onion, parsley, garlic)

For a 6-egg omelette add to the eggs before cooking them ½ cup diced ham, lightly browned in butter, 1 medium onion, chopped and cooked in butter until soft, 1 tablespoon chopped parsley, and 1 small clove of garlic, chopped. Make the omelette in the usual way, but instead of folding it slide it out flat on a round platter and serve.

HAM   MRS. WATERS' OMELETTE
(Ham, cheese, mint, cream)

Add 2 tablespoons chopped ham, 1 tablespoon grated Parmesan cheese, 1 teaspoon chopped mint, and 2 to 3 tablespoons heavy cream to 4 eggs beaten for an omelette. Season with a little pepper and make the omelette in the usual way, folding out on an oval platter. Original and good.

HAM   OMELETTE À LA VIACROZE
(Ham, mushrooms, onion, parsley)

Add to 6 eggs, beaten for an omelette, 1 onion, chopped and cooked soft in butter, and 1 tablespoon of chopped parsley. Cook 3 mushrooms, sliced, in butter until slightly softened and add to them an equal quantity of diced ham and 2 tablespoons of concentrated stock, or meat extract dissolved with a little hot water.

Make 1 flat omelette with half your eggs and slide it onto a plate. Cover with the mushroom and ham combination, and place on this another round omelette made with the remaining eggs. Quite a sandwich!

HAM   OMELETTE AIROLAISE
(Ham, tomato, Swiss cheese, herbs, and wine)

Sauté 2 tablespoons of finely diced lean ham in 1 tablespoon of butter with 2 chopped shallots for about 5 minutes. Add one peeled and seeded tomato, chopped coarsely, 1 teaspoon finely chopped parsley, salt, pepper, and 2 tablespoons of white wine. Cook together for 5 minutes. Rub the bowl with a cut clove of garlic before beating 6 eggs for an omelette, adding 1 tablespoon of grated Swiss cheese to the eggs with the salt and pepper.

Make the omelette in the usual way, spreading the ham and tomato mixture in the center before folding out on the platter.

HAM   OMELETTE NIVERNAISE
(Ham, sorrel, onion)

Sauté in 1 tablespoon of butter, and on both sides, 3 or 4 thin slices of cooked ham. Add about 6 leaves of sorrel, cut up with scissors, and 1 teaspoon of chopped chives or young spring onion. When the sorrel has softened and there is no liquid left in the pan, pour in the beaten, seasoned eggs, stir once or twice, and allow the eggs to set. Serve in the pan like a *tortino*.

HAM   ITALIAN PROSCIUTTO OMELETTE
(Creamed Italian ham, Swiss cheese)

Two thin slices of smoked Italian ham (*prosciutto*) are cut in fine strips and mixed with ½ cup of thick cream sauce. This is made by blending 1 tablespoon of flour into 1 tablespoon of melted butter and adding gradually ½ cup of whole milk, salt, and pepper. Simmer all together about 1 minute.
Beat and season 4 eggs and make as many small omelettes as possible, using 3 tablespoons of the egg mixture for each. Spread them flat on a board and fill the center of each omelette with a little of the ham mixture. Roll them up and place them side by side in a shallow baking dish. Pour ¾ of a cup of milk over them and on top place thin slices of Swiss cheese. Cook in a hot oven until the cheese is melted.

KIDNEY   MADEIRA KIDNEY OMELETTE
(Kidneys, stock, Madeira wine, parsley, tomato sauce)

Cut 2 or 3 lamb kidneys or ½ a veal kidney into ½-inch dice, discarding hard centers. Sauté for 3 minutes in 1 tablespoon of butter. If the kidneys give off much liquid, discard this and then add a little more butter. Sprinkle on 1 teaspoon of flour, allow to brown a little, and blend in 3 tablespoons of meat stock, 1 tablespoon Madeira wine, salt and pepper, and 1 teaspoon chopped parsley. Fold the kidneys into the center of a 6-egg omelette and surround with a ring of tomato sauce (see page 175).

KIDNEY   OMELETTE VILLERANDOISE
(Kidneys, shallot, parsley, white wine)

Cut ½ a veal kidney into ½-inch dice, discarding hard center. Sauté for 3 minutes in 1 tablespoon butter, sprinkle on 1 teaspoon of flour and blend. Brown slightly and season with salt and pepper. Add 1 small chopped shallot and 1 teaspoon chopped parsley. In a small saucepan reduce ¾ cup of dry white wine to about half. Add this to the kidneys, simmer a minute, and fold the mixture into the center of a 6-egg omelette.

KIDNEY   BURGUNDY KIDNEY OMELETTE
(Veal kidneys, mustard sauce)

Cut a veal kidney into small cubes, eliminating all hard parts in the center. Drop these into boiling salted water and parboil a few minutes, or until just done. Do not cook long enough to harden. Make a mustard sauce as follows: melt 1 tablespoon of butter in an enamel or glass saucepan. (For cooking with mustard, avoid aluminum or other metals.) Blend in 1 tablespoon of flour and add gradually ¾ cup of hot stock, salt and pepper, and a pinch of cayenne. Cook for 3 minutes. Add 1 liqueur glass of brandy and cook 4 minutes more. Mix 1 teaspoon of powdered mustard with 1 teaspoon of tarragon vinegar (or use 2 teaspoons of French mixed mustard). Mix the mustard with 1 egg yolk, blend in a little of the stock till liquefied, return this to the rest of the stock, put all over a low heat, or in a double boiler, and reheat, stirring with a wooden spoon. Combine with the veal kidneys. Make a 6- to 8-egg omelette. Fold out and cut a slit in the top. Spoon part of the kidney mixture into the slit and the rest along the side.

LAMB   OMELETTE POLONAISE
(Leftover roast lamb, tomatoes)

Put ½ to ¾ cup of cold cooked lamb through the meat grinder, or if you prefer, cut it up into very small dice with a knife. Heat this with 3 or 4 tablespoons of leftover gravy from the roast, or other meat juice. Fill a 6-egg omelette with the meat and when folded out on the platter, spread on top 2 tomatoes which have been peeled, emptied of their seeds, cut in small bits, and sautéed in 1 tablespoon of butter until soft and thick.

LIVER   CALVES' LIVER OMELETTE
(Calves' liver, cèpes)

Beat 6 eggs for an omelette, adding 1 teaspoon of chopped fresh tarragon leaves with the other seasonings.
Wash thoroughly 3 canned cèpes. Dry them and slice in thin slices. Cut 2 ounces of fresh calves' liver in small thin squares and sauté them quickly and briefly together with the cèpes in 1 tablespoon of butter. Add salt and pepper and turn the pieces until lightly cooked on all sides. Add 1 crushed clove of garlic and cook 1 minute longer. Add a little butter to the

pan, pour in the eggs, stir all together once or twice, and allow the eggs to set. Fold out on a platter or serve flat like a *frittata*.

MEAT MIXTURES   MINIATURE MEAT OMELETTES
(Chicken or veal, ham, mushrooms, cream sauce, cheese)

Dice finely enough cooked leftover chicken or veal to fill 1 cup and cut into fine julienne enough ham to make ½ cup. Add to the meat ¼ pound sliced mushrooms which have been cooked in 1 tablespoon butter for 4 to 5 minutes. Make 1 cup of cream sauce and blend ½ of this with the meat and mushroom mixture.

Mix 6 eggs as for an omelette and make a series of small omelettes in your tiny pan using 3 good tablespoons of beaten egg for each. Fill each omelette with a little of the meat mixture, roll them up, and place them side by side in a buttered oven dish. Pour the remaining cream sauce over the top, sprinkle with Parmesan cheese, and cook in a hot oven until golden brown, which will take about 10 minutes.

MEAT MIXTURES   MEAT AND VEGETABLE
                        CASSEROLE OMELETTE
(Cold meat, onion, tomato, stock, herbs, potato)

❀ *This dish is not strictly an omelette, being baked in the oven in a small casserole.*

Sauté 1 medium onion, sliced, in 1 tablespoon oil combined with 2 tablespoons butter. When soft and golden, add 2 fresh tomatoes which have been peeled, emptied of their seeds, and diced. Add ½ cup of stock, salt and pepper, and 1 teaspoon fresh marjoram (or ½ teaspoon dried marjoram). Simmer

together for 15 minutes and add 1½ cups diced leftover
chicken, veal, beef, or other cooked meat, and 3 medium
sized diced boiled potatoes. Cook all together 3 or 4 minutes.
Separate 4 eggs and beat the yolks thoroughly with salt and
pepper. Beat the whites until stiff and fold into the yolks.

The meat and vegetable mixture is placed in the bottom of a
greased casserole, the eggs poured on top, and the dish is
baked about 8 or 10 minutes in a moderately hot oven, or
until the eggs are golden.

MEAT MIXTURES   HASH OMELETTE (1)
(Chopped meat, bread crumbs, herbs)

❀ *The perfect use for leftover meat—this is no ordinary
hash.*

Either grind or mince finely ¾ cup cooked leftover meat.
Beef, veal, lamb, or pork will do equally well. Soak about ½
cup of coarse bread crumbs with enough milk to moisten
throughout and combine this with the meat, salt and pepper,
a pinch of nutmeg, 1 finely chopped shallot, and 1 teaspoon
chopped parsley.

Combine this mixture with 6 eggs beaten for an omelette and
cook it on both sides. Serve flat like a *frittata* and pass separately a little white sauce containing capers.

MEAT MIXTURES   HASH OMELETTE (2)
(Chopped meat, onions)

Put through the grinder enough cold roast meat to make ¾
of a cup (beef, veal, lamb, or chicken). Sauté 1 tablespoon of
chopped onion in 1 tablespoon of butter until soft, add the
meat, and a pinch each of salt, pepper, cinnamon, and nut-

meg. Blend in 1 teaspoon of flour and add 4 tablespoons of juices left from a roast, or good stock. Heat and stir for about 3 minutes and fold the mixture into the center of a 6-egg omelette. When folded out on the platter, surround the omelette with tiny onions sautéed in butter until soft.

MEAT MIXTURES   MEAT AND VEGETABLE
                                                 FRITTATA
(Cooked meat, vegetables, and cheese)

✿ *All the ingredients for a full meal are in this one dish.* For this omelette use 2 cups of any good leftover meat and vegetables. These are chopped finely together. Brown 1 small chopped onion in 2 tablespoons of oil and add the chopped meat and vegetables, heating and mixing all together.
Beat 6 eggs for an omelette and mix in the meat and vegetables. Heat 3 tablespoons of oil in the omelette pan, pour in the omelette mixture, and cook until lightly browned on the bottom. Turn over on a plate, add a little more oil to the pan if necessary, and slide the omelette back into the pan to brown the other side. Slide out on a round serving dish and sprinkle with grated Parmesan or Romano cheese.

MEAT MIXTURES   OMELETTE MONSELET
(Ham, chicken, tomatoes, mushrooms, Mornay sauce)

✿ *This omelette is named for a celebrated Breton writer and gastronome, who seems to have had a nicely balanced sense of economy combined with taste. Leftovers are here used to make a really dressy dish.*
Mix ⅓ cup of ground cooked ham and ⅓ cup of ground cooked white meat of chicken. In a small saucepan melt 1

tablespoon of butter, blend in 1 tablespoon of flour, salt, and
pepper, and stir in gradually ⅜ cup of cream and several
tablespoons of chicken stock, or a little meat extract. Simmer
and stir until thickened and combine with the ground meats.
When well heated and blended, spread the mixture in the
center of a 6-egg omelette and fold out on an oval ovenproof
platter. Pour over the top ½ cup of Mornay sauce (see page
173), sprinkle with Parmesan cheese and brown lightly under
a hot broiler. At each end of the platter place a mound of
creamed mushrooms and at the sides a row of small broiled
tomatoes.

MEAT MIXTURES   CHINESE OMELETTE (1)
                                        (Eggs Foo Yung)
(Meat, onion, water chestnuts, bean sprouts)

Beat 8 eggs with ¾ cup of water. To them add ½ cup of
finely shredded onion, ¾ cup of ham, chicken, or any cooked
meat, chopped, ½ cup of sliced water chestnuts, 1½ cups of
bean sprouts, and 1 tablespoon of soya sauce. Make 6 separate
omelettes of this mixture in a small pan, heating a spoonful
of oil in the pan each time before pouring the mixture in with
a ladle. Cook on both sides. Serve with Chinese sauce (see
page 171).
(Shrimp, lobster, or crab meat may be used instead of meat
to make eggs Foo Yung.)

MEAT MIXTURE   CHINESE OMELETTE (2)
                                        (Eggs Foo Yung)
(Meat, onions, bean sprouts)

Beat 6 eggs with 6 tablespoons of water, salt, and pepper, or
a little soya sauce.

Chop 6 scallions, or young green onions, and sauté them in butter 3 to 4 minutes. Add 1¼ cups of bean sprouts and 3 cups of raw meat (pork, beef, or chicken) cut in very thin narrow strips or shreds. Stir and continue cooking until the meat is done.

Pour 2 to 3 tablespoons of the beaten egg into a very small pan in which a little oil has been heated. On this, place 2 tablespoons of the meat and vegetable mixture, then ladle on 2 more tablespoons of egg. Cook this little pancake on both sides and repeat the operation until you have used all the ingredients.

PORK   SIAMESE STUFFED OMELETTE
(Pork, peanuts, onion, soya sauce)

Heat 2 cloves of chopped garlic in 2 tablespoons of lard or oil. Add ½ pound of ground lean pork and 15 to 20 chopped, roasted peanuts and cook until the meat is almost done. Add 2 small onions, thinly sliced, 2 teaspoons of sugar, 1½ teaspoons of soya sauce, and a dash of freshly ground pepper.
Beat and season 6 eggs and make two thin omelettes of them, in a large pan, cooking each in 1 tablespoon of oil. Place half the meat mixture in the center of each and fold the four sides to the center to make a square.

PORK   INDOCHINESE PORK AND SHRIMP
                                        OMELETTE
(Pork, shrimps, onion, mushrooms, mussels, and herbs)

Cut ½ pound of fresh lean pork in small dice and cook it in 2 tablespoons of oil together with ¾ cup chopped onion and a good dash of cayenne pepper. When the pork and onions have browned, add ½ cup of stock, cover, and simmer for 20 minutes. Add 1 cup of fresh sliced mushrooms, ½ cup of cooked, peeled, and chopped shrimps, 1 teaspoon of chopped fresh basil, 2 teaspoons of chopped fresh mint, a pinch of sage, freshly ground black pepper, and salt. Cook together for 5 minutes. At the end add 2 dozen fresh mussels with outer "beard" removed. Stir and cook for 3 minutes more.

Add this mixture to 8 beaten eggs and make 4 thin omelettes, cooked in oil or lard, in a rather large pan, turning them to cook on both sides. With them serve fluffy rice and soya sauce.

OMELETTE À LA BERCY

SAUSAGE
(Sausage, herbs)

Make this omelette according to the recipe for Omelette aux Fines Herbes, adding chopped parsley, chives, and any fresh green herbs of your choice to the eggs, and before folding fill it with 6 small broiled pork sausages, *chipolatas,* or others as you prefer. A ring of tomato sauce will add to its savor.

SAUSAGE OMELETTE PARISIENNE

SAUSAGE
(Sausage, mushrooms, onion)

Sauté in butter 1 onion, sliced, and 2 or 3 mushrooms, sliced. Add these to the eggs before making your omelette. Fold it out on the platter and surround it with small broiled sausages.

SAUSAGE OMELETTE FILLIPINI

SAUSAGE
(Sausages, Madeira sauce)

Fill your omelette with small pork sausages which have been skinned before cooking. Over the folded omelette pour ⅓ cup of Madeira sauce (see page 173).

SAUSAGE   BASQUE SAUSAGE OMELETTE
(Sausages, garlic, sweet pepper)

Broil 4 or 5 little *chipolata* sausages in a pan and when done,
cut them in pieces, add 1 chopped clove of garlic and ½ a
sweet red pepper, chopped, to the pan, which should contain
enough fat from the sausages to cook the omelette. Simmer
1 or 2 minutes and pour your 6 beaten, seasoned eggs into the
pan. Stir all together once or twice and allow the eggs to set.

SAUSAGE   OMELETTE DE LA ROUZILLE
(Smoked sausage, herbs, cheese)

A favorite in Perigord is this omelette, which has a little
grated nutmeg and 1 tablespoon of fresh chopped herbs
added to the seasoning when beating the eggs. It should be
cooked in goose or pork fat and sprinkled with grated cheese
after folding. Surround it with thin slices of large smoked
sausage and serve.

SAUSAGE   SAUSAGE OMELETTE LORRAINE
(Frankfort sausage, onion, tomato sauce)

Add 1 large onion, sliced and sautéed, and 1 tablespoon
finely chopped parsley, salt, and pepper to the 6 eggs when
beating them. Make a flat, rather soft omelette with half your
eggs, and on this, place a layer of broiled, sliced Frankfort
sausage (or other of this type), skinned before cooking. Make
a second flat omelette with the rest of your eggs, place it on
top, and surround with a ring of tomato sauce.

SAUSAGE   OMELETTE NANCÉENNE
(Blood sausage, onion, parsley)

Beat 6 eggs for an omelette, adding salt, pepper, 1 teaspoon
of finely chopped parsley, and 1 chopped onion sautéed in 1
tablespoon of butter until soft. Make two flat omelettes of this
mixture. Place one on the serving platter and cover it with
slices of blood sausage sautéed in butter. Place the second
omelette on top and over all pour 2 tablespoons of browned
butter combined with ½ teaspoon of meat extract. Sprinkle
with chopped parsley and serve.

SAUSAGE   VIENNESE SAUSAGE OMELETTE
(Sausage, bacon, potatoes, peas, chives)

Broil ¼ pound of saugases in a saucepan. Remove and brown
1 or 2 thinly sliced cooked potatoes in the fat from the sausages. Broil 6 slices of bacon and drain. Beat 6 eggs with salt
and pepper, ½ teaspoon of chopped chives, and ¼ cup
cooked green peas. Make 2 omelettes of the egg mixture and
place half the filling in each. Fold out and serve.

SWEETBREADS   OMELETTE À LA TALLEYRAND
(Fried sweetbreads, onion, curry, cream sauce)

❀ *If Talleyrand had anything to do with this, he was more
   than a statesman.*
Add to the eggs when beating them 1 large onion, chopped
and sautéed in butter, ½ teaspoon of curry, salt, and pepper.
Make this omelette flat and surround it with slices of par-

boiled sweetbreads, which have been dipped in beaten egg and breadcrumbs and fried in butter. On the slices of sweetbread distribute discreetly about ½ cup of cream sauce (see page 172) made with pure cream and a minimum of flour.

SWEETBREADS   SWEETBREAD OMELETTE MAÎTRE
                                                        D'HÔTEL
(Sweetbreads, kidney, lemon juice, parsley)

Sauté in 2 tablespoons butter ½ cup of diced parboiled sweetbreads and ½ cup of diced veal kidneys. Cook quickly, allowing the butter to brown a little. Sprinkle in ½ teaspoon of lemon juice and 1 teaspoon finely chopped parsley. Fill a 6-egg omelette with this mixture and turn out on a platter.

TONGUE   OMELETTE DUCHESSE À L'ECARLATE
(Beef tongue, chicken, mushrooms, cheese, bread, cream sauce, Madeira sauce)

Beat up 8 eggs with 1 tablespoon concentrated chicken stock, 2 tablespoons cream, 1 tablespoon grated Swiss or Parmesan cheese, salt, pepper, a pinch of paprika, and a pinch of nutmeg. With this mixture make 8 or 10 separate small omelettes. It is best to make half at a time, filling the first 4 or 5 little omelettes and keeping them warm while preparing the rest.

Mix 1½ cups minced, cooked chicken with 3 or 4 mushrooms, chopped and sautéed in butter, and enough well seasoned rich cream sauce to hold them together. Fill each little omelette with this mixture and fold it up.

Butter 5 slices of bread and toast them under the broiler. On each slice of toast place an equal sized thin slice of cooked beef tongue heated in a little butter. On each of these place 2 tiny omelettes and spread on each a spoonful of hot Madeira sauce (see page 173). A sprinkling of finely chopped fresh parsley and the dish is ready for the Duchess and fit for a queen.

VEAL   OMELETTE MOURTERADE
(Roast veal)

Leftover roast veal may be cut into small dice and browned in goose fat or other good fat to fill a plain omelette. Moisten with some of the juices left from the roast just before filling the omelette.

VEGETABLE OMELETTES

VEGETABLE OMELETTES

ARTICHOKE

ARTICHOKE OMELETTE PROVENÇALE

(Artichokes, lemon juice)

❄ *This resembles the Florentine* tortino *which is cooked and served in the same gratin dish. In Italy a special variety of tender small artichoke is used. These are difficult to obtain in this country, but the center part of any artichoke, if young enough, and with choke removed, can be very good. These may be parboiled first if desired.*

Remove the outer leaves and chokes from very young artichokes, cut off the tips of the other leaves, cut the artichokes in extremely thin vertical slices, rub with a little lemon juice, and cook them slowly in a little olive oil, covered, until tender.

Beat the eggs for the omelette, season, and pour over the artichokes in the pan, adding first a little more oil or some butter, should this be necessary. Mingle together and as soon as the eggs are set serve in the same dish.

ARTICHOKE

OMELETTE WITH ARTICHOKE BOTTOMS

(Artichokes, cream sauce)

Slice the bottoms of 2 cooked artichokes, heat them in butter, and stir in 2 tablespoons thick cream sauce (see page 172).

Fold this into the center of a 6-egg omelette, place fried triangles of bread at each side and a little of the cream sauce along the top.

ARTICHOKE   OMELETTE DURAND
(Artichoke bottoms, truffle, mushrooms)

❀ *The next time you serve artichokes, reserve one of the*
   bases and use it in the following delicious manner.
Sauté in 1 tablespoon butter 2 or 3 mushrooms, sliced, and when the mushrooms are partly cooked, add 1 cooked artichoke bottom, sliced, and 1 truffle, sliced. Season with salt and pepper and stir in 2 tablespoons of meat juices made by dissolving ½ teaspoon of meat glaze or extract in 4 tablespoons of water or stock. Fill a 6-egg omelette with this delicious mixture.

ARTICHOKE   OMELETTE DU JARDINIER
(Artichoke, mushrooms, herbs, tomato sauce)

Remove the outer leaves of a small, tender young artichoke, trim the tops of the other leaves, and slice vertically in thin slices, removing the choke. Cook these slices in oil, slowly, until done. Remove the artichoke slices and in the same pan cook 3 or 4 mushrooms, sliced, until all liquid has evaporated. Mix artichokes and mushrooms with 1 teaspoon of parsley, chives, and tarragon chopped together. Rub a bowl with garlic before beating up 6 eggs for the omelette, which you fill with this mixture. A little tomato sauce on the side is the finishing touch.

ARTICHOKE   OMELETTE À L'ALGÉRIENNE
(Artichoke bottoms, tomato sauce)

Sauté 2 cooked artichoke bottoms, sliced, in 1 tablespoon butter and mingle with the eggs before making the omelette.
Around the omelette, after folding it out on the platter, pour
a ring of tomato sauce (see page 175). If preferred, place the
artichoke bottoms, halved, around the omelette on the platter.

ARTICHOKE   FRITTATA WITH ARTICHOKE
(Artichoke, bread crumbs, garlic, herbs, and cheese)

Remove outer leaves and chokes of 2 or 3 small, very young
artichokes, and slice vertically in very thin slices. Heat 3 tablespoons of oil in a frying pan, add the slices of artichoke, a little salt and pepper, cover and cook slowly, turning often, until they are tender. This may take 20 minutes to half an hour.
Beat lightly 4 eggs, together with salt and pepper, 1 clove of
chopped garlic, 2 slices of stale bread soaked in a little water
and pressed dry, ½ teaspon of marjoram, and 2 tablespoons of
grated Parmesan cheese. Add the cooked artichokes and mix
all together.
Heat 2 tablespoons of oil in the omelette pan, pour in the
mixture, and cook slowly 5 to 8 minutes on each side, adding
more oil if necessary.

ASPARAGUS   OMELETTE WITH ASPARAGUS TIPS
(Fresh asparagus)

Peel and dice 4 or 5 stalks of asparagus, reserving the tips in
2-inch lengths. Drop the diced bits into boiling water for 3 or

4 minutes. Remove from the water with a skimmer. Cook the tips 5 to 6 minutes. Reheat the diced asparagus in butter, salt, and pepper and mix it with the eggs when making your omelette. Place the tips in a neatly arranged bunch on top of your folded omelette and pour over them 1 tablespoon of melted butter. You may use leftover cooked asparagus in the same way, cutting it up and heating it in butter before making the omelette.

ASPARAGUS   OMELETTE ARGENTEUIL
(Fresh asparagus, cream sauce)

Cut 2½-inch tips from 1½ pounds of asparagus, cut these in half again, and drop them into boiling salted water. Cook for 5 to 6 minutes, drain, and heat them in 1 tablespoon butter. Mix the asparagus with ½ cup of cream sauce (see page 172) and fold into the center of a 6-egg omelette.

ASPARAGUS   ENGLISH ASPARAGUS OMELETTE
(Fresh asparagus, herbs, cream sauce with egg)

❀ *This old recipe dates from 1685 and was called "An*
   Amlet of Asparagus." It is just as good today, no matter
   how you spell it.

Peel and dice 4 or more stalks of asparagus, drop in boiling salted water for 3 or 4 minutes. Drain and sauté the pieces in 1 tablespoon of butter to finish cooking. Season and sprinkle over them 1 teaspoon parsley and chives chopped together. Beat up 1 egg yolk with 3 tablespoons of cream, a generous pinch each of salt and pepper, and stir this into the asparagus over a very low fire, just until it begins to thicken, being care-

ful not to allow the egg to coagulate. Pour this delicately delicious mixture over your folded omelette on the platter.

ASPARAGUS   OMELETTE ANDRÉ-THEURIET
(*Morels* or mushrooms, asparagus, Supreme sauce, truffles)

✤ *This is a truly dressy and delicious omelette to present to*
   your guests. It calls for the most exquisite of all the
   mushroom family, morels. *But if these are unobtainable,*
   good white mushrooms will do.

Cook ½ pound of *morels* or small white mushrooms in 2 tablespoons of butter with a few drops of lemon juice, salt, and
pepper. Cut 2½-inch tips from 1½ pounds of asparagus (or
use a package of frozen asparagus tips) and steam them about
20 minutes, or until tender. Drain the asparagus and heat in
1 tablespoon of butter. Make a Supreme sauce (see page 174).
Mix half of the sauce with the mushrooms and fill the omelette with this. When folded out neatly on the platter, place
on top a row of sliced truffles heated in butter, a bouquet of
asparagus tips on each side, and spoon the rest of the sauce
over these.

ASPARAGUS   PURÉE OF ASPARAGUS OMELETTE
(Asparagus, seasonings)

Drain 1 pint of canned asparagus tips and drop them in boiling water. After 2 minutes drain them from the water and
mash through a fine sieve. Season with salt, a few grains of
cayenne, and ½ teaspoon of sugar. Add 1 tablespoon of butter and heat, stirring, for about 5 minutes. Place half the

asparagus purée in the center of a plain omelette, and spread the rest along the side after folding it out on the platter.

BEANS   STRING BEAN OMELETTE
(String beans, cream, tomato sauce)

For this omelette use fresh string beans (or leftovers), about 1 cup, cut into short pieces and boiled in salted water. Drain, add a lump of butter and 1 tablespoon of heavy cream. Season with a pinch of nutmeg, heat, and fill your omelette with the beans. A little tomato sauce on each side adds interest.

BROCCOLI   FRITTATA WITH BROCCOLI
(Broccoli, garlic, cheese)

Cut 2 to 3 stalks of cooked broccoli in 1-inch pieces and combine them with 6 beaten eggs. Add salt and pepper, 1 clove of garlic, chopped, and 2 to 3 tablespoons of grated Parmesan cheese. Heat 2 tablespoons of oil in your omelette pan, pour in the mixture, and cook slowly for 5 to 8 minutes on each side, adding more oil if necessary.

BRUSSELS SPROUTS   OMELETTE BRUXELLOISE
(Brussels sprouts, meat juice)

Fresh or leftover brussels sprouts will do, and the smaller they are, the better. Sauté ¾ cups of cooked brussels sprouts in butter until slightly browned. Add 1 tablespoon of meat juices from a roast, or a bit of meat extract dissolved in water, to the brussels sprouts before folding into the center of the omelette.

CARROTS   OMELETTE À LA VICHY
(Carrots, meat juice)

Heat ¾ cup leftover cooked carrots in 1 tablespoon bouillon
with 1 teaspoon butter to fill this omelette, or cook fresh carrots in the Vichy style as follows: the carrots are scraped,
thinly sliced, and braised in a heavy covered saucepan over a
low fire with a slice of onion, a sprig of parsley, a pinch of
thyme, a pinch of sugar, salt and pepper, a lump of butter,
and several tablespoons of stock. When soft and all liquid
evaporated, remove the onion and parsley and fill the omelette
with the carrots.

CARROTS   OMELETTE CRÉCY
(Carrots, cream sauce)

When beating the eggs, add ½ cup of grated carrots cooked
until soft in the Vichy manner (see Omelette Vichy). When
serving the omelette, pour several tablespoons of cream sauce
(see page 172) over the top. Another version of this is made
by mashing the carrots to a purée which is folded into the center of the omelette. Arrange a row of round cooked carrot
slices on top. Pour a little cream sauce over them and serve.

CAULIFLOWER   CAULIFLOWER OMELETTE (1)
(Cauliflower, cream, cheese)

Press a small cooked cauliflower through a fine sieve, add salt,
pepper, a little grated nutmeg, 1 tablespoon of butter, and 2
egg yolks beaten up with 2 or 3 tablespoons of heavy cream.
Reheat, stirring continually, until the purée thickens a little.

Place half the mixture in the center of a 6-egg omelette and spread the rest on top after folding out. Sprinkle with Parmesan cheese and brown lightly under a hot broiler.

CAULIFLOWER   CAULIFLOWER OMELETTE (2)
(Cauliflower, seasonings)

Break off about 1 cup of cauliflower flowerets and steam until cooked but not too soft. Sauté these in 2 tablespoons of melted butter, tossing to cook all sides, season with salt and pepper, and fold them into the center of a 6-egg omelette.
Leftover cooked cauliflower may be used in this way.

CELERIAC   OMELETTE MONTBRY
(Celeriac, horseradish, herbs, Mornay sauce)

Beat 6 eggs with salt and pepper, 1 teaspoon of horseradish, 1 teaspoon chopped parsley, and ½ teaspoon chopped chives. Make 2 thin omelettes of this mixture. On the first one spread ¾ cup diced cooked celeriac (celery root) mixed with ⅓ cup cream sauce (see page 172). Place the second omelette on top and pour over it ½ cup Mornay sauce (see page 173). Sprinkle with grated Parmesan cheese and a little melted butter and brown lightly under a hot broiler.

CÈPES   OMELETTE WITH CÈPES
(Cèpes, parsley)

Drain a small can of cèpes. Rinse and dry thoroughly 4 or 5 of these large fungi and slice them finely. Cook briskly in 2 or 3 tablespoons of hot oil turning them over several times. After

4 or 5 minutes add salt and 1 teaspoon of chopped parsley. Drop in 6 beaten, seasoned eggs and stir all together with the flat side of a fork. When done, fold out on a platter, or if you find this difficult, serve from the pan in which the omelette was cooked. A little chopped garlic may be added to the *cèpes* while cooking if you like.

CHESTNUTS
(Chestnuts, stock)

OMELETTE À LA CHATELAINE

Peel and parboil 6 large chestnuts (*marrons*) and when almost cooked, drain, break up into bits, and sauté them in 1 tablespoon of butter. When slightly browned, add 1 tablespoon of meat juice or stock, simmer several minutes, season with a pinch of salt and pepper and fold into the center of a 6-egg omelette. A little cream sauce (see page 172) over the top is a welcome addition.

CORN
(Corn, cream sauce)

CREAMED CORN OMELETTE

Scrape the kernels from 2 ears of cold, boiled corn and combine with about ¼ cup rich cream sauce (see page 172), or just enough to give a nice consistency. Reheat, season well, and fold into the center of a 6-egg omelette.

CORN
(Corn)

MOUSSELINE CORN OMELETTE

Grate off finely the kernels from 2 to 3 ears of cold boiled corn. Beat the yolks and whites of 6 eggs separately as for a mousseline omelette. Mix the corn with the yolks, adding salt and pepper and 1 tablespoon of heavy cream. Blend yolks and whites carefully and proceed as for a mousseline omelette.

CUCUMBER   OMELETTE MONTENEGRO
(Cucumber, ham)

Peel 1 small cucumber, slit it lengthwise, and scoop out the seeds. Slice into thin slices, drop these into boiling salted water, and boil for 3 minutes. Drain and dry them on a cloth. Melt 1½ tablespoons of butter in a frying pan and in this sauté 2 tablespoons of diced cooked ham and the cucumbers. Toss over a good heat for 5 or 6 minutes. Add 1 teaspoon finely chopped parsley, combine the mixture with 6 beaten eggs, and make your omelette in the usual way.

CUCUMBER   OMELETTE CZARINA
(Cucumber, sour cream)

 Are you willing to learn something from the Russians? From the old regime, anyway . . .
Peel a cucumber, slice it in two lengthwise, and scoop out the seeds. Cut in dice and sauté gently in 1 tablespoon of butter until soft. Add salt and pepper, a very light sprinkling of flour, and blend in 3 tablespoons of sour cream. Simmer 1 minute and fold into the center of a 6-egg omelette. Pour a little Supreme sauce (see page 174) along the sides and serve.

EGGPLANT   EGGPLANT OMELETTE NIÇOISE
(Eggplant, zucchini, herbs, cheese)

Peel and cut ½ a small eggplant into finger-sized pieces. Slice 1 small zucchini (Italian squash) and put both together into a saucepan with 1 tablespoon of hot oil and 1 tablespoon of butter. Cover and braise over a low fire. When soft, chop them fairly finely and add salt and pepper and 1 teaspoon of chopped parsley and chervil combined. When making your 6-egg omelette add salt, pepper, 1 tablespoon of grated Parmesan cheese, and a good pinch of nutmeg and a little cinnamon to the eggs. Blend the vegetables with the eggs in the pan and when set, finish cooking the top under the broiler. Serve from the pan.

EGGPLANT   OMELETTE MISTRAL
(Eggplant, tomato, garlic, parsley)

Make this omelette in the pan in which it is to be served, if you so desire.
Peel and cut in dice ½ an eggplant and sauté in 2 tablespoons of oil and 1 tablespoon of butter. Add 2 tomatoes, peeled, seeded, and cut in dice. When the liquid has disappeared, add salt and pepper, 1 chopped clove of garlic, and 1 tablespoon of chopped parsley. When the vegetables are thoroughly soft, pour in 6 beaten, seasoned eggs, stir together, and make a flat round omelette.

EGGPLANT   SLICED EGGPLANT OMELETTE
(Fried eggplant, tomato sauce)

Place along the top of a plain folded omelette overlapping slices of eggplant fried in butter, sprinkle with chopped parsley, surround with tomato sauce, and serve.

ENDIVE   OMELETTE FLAMANDE

Slice finely 3 heads of endive and sauté gently in butter until soft. Season with salt and pepper, sprinkle with ½ teaspoon of flour, add 4 tablespoons of heavy cream, and simmer until thickened. Fold into the center of a 6-egg omelette.

FENNEL   FENNEL OMELETTE
(Fresh fennel, parsley, garlic)

Mince the feathery leaves of 2 fennel plants, or enough to make about 1½ cups. To this add 1 teaspoon chopped parsley and 1 clove of garlic, chopped. Sauté these in 1 tablespoon of butter, stirring and blending together. When softened, add 1 tablespoon of butter to the pan, pour on 6 beaten, seasoned eggs, stir all together, and when half cooked, flip over and brown lightly on the other side. Serve flat on a round platter.

HERBS   OMELETTE AUX FINES HERBES
(Parsley, chives, tarragon, chervil)

❀ *This is the classic, basic, and altogether delicious ome-
    lette aux fines herbes.*
Season 6 eggs with salt and pepper, add 3 teaspoons of water, and beat with a fork no more than 30 seconds. Stir in 2 table-spoons of mixed, finely chopped herbs: parsley, chives, tar-ragon, and chervil. Melt 1 tablespoon of butter in your hot omelette pan but do not allow to brown. Pour in the eggs, give one or two stirs with the flat side of the fork, tilt this way and that to allow the uncooked eggs to run under, and when cooked, but still soft on top, slide to the side of the pan away

from the handle. Fold over the side nearest the handle with a spatula, slip the other side onto the platter held in the right hand, turn the pan over completely on the platter, thus turning the omelette out neatly folded in three, perfectly cooked but soft in the center.

HERBS   ANOTHER OMELETTE AUX FINES HERBES
(Shallot, mushrooms, parsley)

Chop finely 2 shallots and sauté them gently in 1 tablespoon of butter for 1 or 2 minutes. Add 3 chopped mushrooms and 1 tablespoon chopped parsley. Cook 1 or 2 minutes more and stir into the beaten eggs before making your omelette.

HERBS   ITALIAN FRITTATA WITH HERBS
(Mint, basil)

Beat 6 eggs with salt and pepper, 1 tablespoon of chopped fresh mint, and ¾ tablespoon of chopped fresh basil. Cook slowly in 1 tablespoon of butter until brown on one side, add more butter before turning to cook the other side.

HERBS   GERMAN OMELETTE WITH HERBS
(Parsley, chives)

When mixing the batter for German omelettes (see page 22), add 1 tablespoon of finely chopped parsley and 1 teaspoon of chopped chives. Excellent with meat or vegetables.

LETTUCE   LETTUCE OMELETTE
(Lettuce, cream sauce)

Slice coarsely a small head of fresh green garden lettuce and
sauté in 1 tablespoon of butter until softened. Season and
combine with a few spoonfuls of cream sauce (see page 172)
before folding into the center of your omelette.

MIXED VEGETABLES   GENOESE FRITTATA
(Onion, artichoke, spinach, and other greens)

Chop finely 1 onion and sauté it in 1 tablespoon of oil combined with ½ tablespoon of butter until soft and transparent.
Slice 2 or 3 small young tender artichokes lengthwise and
boil in salted water until softened. When the artichokes are
almost done add to the boiling water 6 or 8 leaves of spinach
and the same amount of beet greens or other good green vegetable. Cook briefly, drain thoroughly, and chop coarsely. Add
these vegetables, together with the onion, to the beaten eggs
before making the omelette. Pour into the hot butter in the
omelette pan and cook over a moderate fire until set. Do not
turn or fold, but serve "as is." Grated Parmesan cheese may
be sprinkled on top if desired.

MIXED VEGETABLES   ITALIAN OMELETTES WITH
                                        GREENS
(Onion, peas, green pepper, zucchini, tomato)

Slice ½ an onion and sauté in 2 tablespoons oil until softened.
Add ½ cup of cooked peas, 1 medium sized green pepper, cut
in small pieces, 1 small zucchini (Italian squash), cut in

small pieces. Cook slowly for 20 minutes. Now add 1 tomato, peeled, seeded, and diced, ½ teaspoon orégano, salt, and pepper and cook 3 or 4 minutes longer. Stir ½ cup of milk gradually into 2 tablespoons of flour until smooth, add 4 eggs, salt, and pepper, and beat for 5 minutes. In a tiny frying pan put 2 tablespoons of this batter and cook slowly until set. Place 1 tablespoon of the vegetable mixture upon it and cover with 2 tablespoons of the egg batter. Turn carefully and cook gently on the other side. Remove to a warm platter and repeat until you have used all the batter and vegetables.

MIXED VEGETABLES   OMELETTE À LA JARDINIÈRE
(Carrot, turnip, green beans, potato, peas, asparagus, cauliflower, cream sauce)

Sauté in 2 or more tablespoons of butter ¼ cup each of cooked, diced carrots, white turnip, string beans, potato, and peas. Mix the vegetables with the eggs before making the omelette. Do not fold, but serve flat, placing on top a small bunch of cooked green asparagus tips and a few cooked cauliflower flowerets. Pour a circle of cream sauce (see page 172) on the omelette before serving.

MIXED VEGETABLES   VEGETABLE OMELETTE
                                          BÉARNAISE
(Asparagus, mushrooms, artichoke bottoms, Béarnaise sauce)

Mix gradually with your beaten eggs 3 tablespoons of purée of fresh asparagus made by forcing cooked asparagus through a fine sieve. Sauté 3 mushrooms, sliced, in butter for 3 minutes and add 1 cooked artichoke bottom, sliced. When heated through, fold these vegetables into the center of the asparagus flavored omelette. Surround the omelette with a Béarnaise sauce (see page 171) and serve.

MIXED VEGETABLES   PROVINCIAL BÉARNAISE
                                    OMELETTE
(Bacon, green pepper, capers, tomato purée)

❧ *This omelette is truly named for the province where it originated, whereas the foregoing takes its name from the sauce, which in reality was created in Paris but named for the native province of the great King Henry IV.*

Heat 2 tablespoons diced bacon in a frying pan until lightly browned. Chop 1 medium sized green pepper with 1 teaspoon sour capers and add to the bacon. When the pepper is softened, add 1 tablespoon of tomato purée, cook all together a few seconds, and stir the mixture into the beaten eggs before making the omelette. Of if you prefer, fold the mixture into the center of the cooked omelette.

MIXED VEGETABLES   SPANISH OMELETTE (1)
(Onion, green pepper, tomatoes, ham)

Slice 1 onion and 1 small sweet green or red pepper and sauté in 1 tablespoon butter combined with 1 tablespoon oil until the vegetables are softened. Add 2 tomatoes, peeled, seeded, and diced, salt, and pepper and cook until all liquid has evaporated and the mixture is thick. Add 1 tablespoon finely slivered ham, heat, and serve the vegetable mixture beside the folded omelette on the platter. This omelette can be made without the ham, or even using tomatoes and peppers alone. This makes a simpler but excellent filling.

MIXED VEGETABLES   SPANISH OMELETTE (2)
(Potato, onion, green pepper, tomatoes)

Cut 1 small boiled potato in cubes and brown in 1 tablespoon
of butter. Chop 1 small onion and 1 small red or green sweet
pepper and add to the pan. When partly cooked, add 1 tomato, peeled, seeded, and diced, salt, and pepper. When all
the vegetables are cooked to a thick consistency, add them to
the egg mixture and make your omelette, turning to cook
both sides. Do not fold, but serve flat.

MIXED VEGETABLES   SPANISH OMELETTE (3)
(Onion, garlic, tomato, mushrooms, green peppers, parsley,
stock)

Sauté 1 sliced onion in 2 tablespoons of oil till soft and
golden. Add 1 small minced clove of garlic and cook 1 minute. Then add 1 large tomato, peeled and chopped, 4 mushrooms, chopped, 1 small sweet pepper, chopped, and simmer
until thick. Add salt and pepper, ½ teaspoon chopped parsley,
2 cups of meat stock (beef or chicken) and simmer down
until thick again. This will take some time as you cannot
hurry the process. Put half of this mixture in the center of
your folded omelette and spoon the rest on to the platter on
each side.

MIXED VEGETABLES   SPANISH OMELETTE (4)
(Tomato, ham)

Sauté 2 tablespoons of finely diced cooked ham in 1 tablespoon of butter until slightly browned. Remove from the pan

and mix the ham with the eggs before making your omelette. Peel and slice 2 firm tomatoes and sauté the slices about 2 minutes on each side in the pan in which you cooked your ham, adding butter if necessary. While still firm enough to handle, season with salt and pepper and remove the slices with a spatula to the center of the omelette, forming an overlapping row. Fold the omelette and serve.

MIXED VEGETABLES   MEXICAN OMELETTE
(Onion, peppers, mushrooms, tomato sauce, garlic, chili)

Melt 4 tablespoons of butter in a frying pan. Add 3 tablespoons of chopped onion, 3 tablespoons of chopped green pepper, 1 cup sliced mushrooms, 1 mashed clove of garlic, salt, and pepper. Cook slowly until soft and lightly browned. Add 1 cup of tomato sauce, 1 teaspoon of chili powder and simmer together about 4 minutes.

Make a 6-egg omelette and pour the above sauce along each side after folding it out on the platter.

MIXED VEGETABLES   ITALIAN COUNTRY FRITTATA
(Zucchini, celery, tomatoes, cheese, basil)

Dice 1 zucchini and 1 heart of celery and cook them slowly in 2 tablespoons of hot oil until they are a little browned. Add 2 fresh peeled and seeded tomatoes which have been cut into large dice. Add salt and pepper and simmer for about 15 minutes. Beat 4 eggs with salt and pepper, 2 tablespoons of grated Parmesan cheese, and 1 teaspoon of chopped fresh basil. Combine eggs and vegetables and cook the *frittata* slowly in

2 tablespoons of oil about 10 minutes on each side, or until browned.

MIXED VEGETABLES   BRAZILIAN OMELETTE (Cold)
(Peas, peppers, potato, onion)

Fry separately, each in a generous tablespoon of butter, ⅓ cup of cooked peas, ¼ cup raw diced sweet pepper, ¼ cup diced, cooked potato, and ¼ cup chopped raw onion. Season each with salt and pepper. Melt 2 generous tablespoons of butter in an omelette pan, break 6 eggs into a bowl, and pour them directly into the hot butter. Mix the vegetables with the eggs immediately and stir all well together. When set, slide out on a plate. This is served cold, cut up in strips.

MIXED VEGETABLES   CHINESE ALMOND OMELETTE
(Almonds, celery, mushrooms, onion, bean sprouts)

❀ *The Chinese have much to teach us about the blending of textures and delicate flavors. These little almond omelettes should be about 3 inches in diameter.*

Slice 1 or 2 stalks of celery very finely on the bias, or enough to make ½ a cup. Slice finely ½ cup of mushrooms and ½ cup of onion. Drop these vegetables, together with 1 cup of bean sprouts, into 2 cups of boiling salted water, boil for 2 minutes, and drain. Beat 4 eggs and add to them the vegetables, ½ cup of salted almonds, salt and pepper, and 1 tablespoon of soya sauce. Make a number of small omelettes with this mixture in your tiniest pan, turning them to brown on each side. Keep warm. Serve with a bowl of dry, flaky, boiled rice and Chinese sauce (see page 171).

MORELS   OMELETTE COMPIÈGNE
(Morels, cream, cinnamon, meat glaze)

Sauté briefly in 1 tablespoon of butter ¼ pound of fresh
morels, if obtainable. Otherwise dried ones which have been
soaked back to their original size, then drained and dried, are
very good. After 3 or 4 minutes pour over them about ¼
cup of heavy cream, add salt, a dash of cinnamon, and 2 tablespoons of chicken or veal glaze. (Condensed juices left
from a roast, and with fat removed, will do for this.) Blend
all together and simmer a minute or two. Fill a 6-egg omelette with this delicate composition, and if you choose to "gild
the lily," spread a little Mornay sauce (see page 173) on top,
sprinkle with grated Parmesan cheese and melted butter, and
brown lightly under a hot broiler. (If your sauce is too liquid,
you may thicken it ever so slightly by sprinkling ½ teaspoon
of potato starch over the morels and blending it in before
adding the cream.)

MUSHROOM   MUSHROOM RUM OMELETTE
(Mushrooms, rum, cream)

Wash, dry, and slice ¼ pound of mushrooms, sprinkle with 1
tablespoon rum or brandy, and let stand 20 minutes. Just before making a 6-egg omelette heat the mushrooms in 1 tablespoon melted butter about 5 minutes, or until most of the
liquid has evaporated. Season with salt and pepper, blend in
2 tablespoons of heavy cream, and reheat. Place the mushrooms in the center of the omelette before folding it.

MUSHROOMS   MUSHROOM HERB OMELETTE
(Mushrooms, herbs)

Wash, dry, and slice ¼ pound of mushrooms and sauté in 1 tablespoon melted butter until the liquid has almost entirely evaporated. Sprinkle over them 1 teaspoon chopped parsley and salt and pepper. Add 1 tablespoon chopped parsley and chives combined to your eggs when beating them, first rubbing the inside of the bowl with a cut end of garlic. Make your omelette and fold the mushrooms into the center. A delicious blending of flavors will result.

MUSHROOMS   CREAM MUSHROOM OMELETTE
(Mushrooms, cream, cheese)

Wash, dry, and slice ¼ pound of mushrooms and sauté in 1 tablespoon butter about 5 minutes. Add salt and pepper and 2 or 3 tablespoons heavy cream and reheat. Fold them into the center of your omelette on an ovenproof oval platter and pour over the top a little Bechamel sauce, made with cream, and to which you have added 1 teaspoon grated Swiss or Parmesan cheese. Sprinkle a little grated cheese on top and place under a hot broiler briefly, or until golden brown.
If to the sautéed mushrooms you add 1 beaten yolk of egg as well as the cream, the result is even more delicious.

MUSHROOMS   OMELETTE CASANOVA
(Mushrooms, cream, curry, cheese)

Chop ¼ pound of mushrooms very finely, sauté in 1 generous tablespoon of butter for several minutes, add salt and pepper, and sprinkle on about ½ teaspoon of flour. When blended, add 2 or 3 tablespoons of cream and cook until unctuous. Fill the center of your omelette with this purée and after folding it out on an ovenproof platter pour a little cream sauce (see page 172) flavored with curry over the top. Sprinkle a little grated Swiss or Parmesan cheese on this and place it under a hot broiler just long enough to gild the top but not long enough to harden the omelette.

MUSHROOMS

MRS. WATERS' MUSHROOM OMELETTE

(Mushrooms, garlic, bread, cheese, marjoram)

❀ *In subtle flavor and texture this mousseline omelette is really a dream.*

Wash, dry, and slice ¼ pound of mushrooms and sauté in 1 tablespoon of melted butter, placing a cut clove of garlic in the pan. Season with salt and pepper and cook about 4 or 5 minutes. Remove the garlic. Beat the yolks and whites of 4 eggs separately until the yolks are creamy and the whites are stiff. Now add to the yolks a small piece of bread (about ½ a slice without crust) which has been crumbled up and soaked in water, as well as 1 tablespoon grated Parmesan cheese, salt and pepper, and ½ teaspoon fresh chopped marjoram (less if dried). Add the whites and beat all together with a fork until the bread is well absorbed throughout. Melt 2 tablespoons of butter in the pan containing the mushrooms and pour in the egg mixture. Mix all well together with a fork and cook over a very moderate heat to avoid the omelette's sticking to the pan. While still creamy on top run a spatula around the edges and underneath, fold in two, and slide out on a platter.

MUSHROOMS

(Creamed mushrooms)

GERMAN OMELETTE WITH MUSHROOMS

Make 2 thin German omelettes according to the basic recipe (see page 22) and before rolling them up spread with mushroom purée made as follows: chop very finely ¾ of a pound of fresh mushrooms, caps and stems together. Sauté in 2 tablespoons of butter until all liquid has evaporated. Season with salt and pepper and a pinch of cayenne. Sprinkle with 1 teaspoon of flour, blend, and stir in ¼ cup heavy cream or chicken stock. When thickened, spread the mixture on the omelettes, roll them up, cut in sections, and serve with meat or other dishes as desired.

ONIONS

(Onions)

PLAIN ONION OMELETTE

Slice thinly 2 medium onions and sauté them slowly over a low fire in 1 generous tablespoon of butter until they are soft and golden. Keep the fire low as they burn easily. Season with salt and pepper and spread them across the center of a 6-egg omelette before folding it.

ONIONS

(Onions, nutmeg, cream sauce)

SAVORY ONION OMELETTE

❀ *In reality this is more like a soufflé than an omelette, but it is a delicious variation on the onion-and-egg theme.* Slice thinly 3 onions and cook them down slowly in 2 tablespoons of butter until soft, being careful not to allow them to brown. Sprinkle on 1 teaspoon of flour, salt, pepper, and a little grated nutmeg. When well blended, stir in 3 tablespoons of cream, or just enough to make the mixture thicken. Allow to cool. When the onions are cold, mix them with 6 thoroughly beaten egg yolks, then fold in the 6 whites, beaten stiff.

This may be cooked in a moderately hot oven in a casserole lined with buttered paper, in which case you turn it out on a round dish and remove the paper, pouring a Bechamel or cream sauce (see page 172) over the top before serving. Or if you prefer, bake as a soufflé and serve in the dish.

ONIONS   ONION OMELETTE WITH CROUTONS
(Onions, bread croutons)

Slice 2 onions and sauté them slowly in 1 generous table-spoon of butter till soft and golden. Cut enough bread into dice to make 3 heaping tablespoons. Brown these very slowly in butter in another pan until golden on all sides, crisp, and delicious. After placing the onions in the center of the ome-lette sprinkle the croutons evenly over them, fold, and serve. Once again we point out the charm of contrasting textures. These crisp, buttery bits are absolutely delicious in the midst of the soft flavorful onions and eggs.

ONIONS   LYONNAISE ONION OMELETTE
(Onions, parsley, vinegar)

Chop finely 1 onion, sauté slowly in butter until soft, and mix it with the beaten eggs, together with 1 tablespoon finely chopped parsley. Make the omelette and when turned out on the platter, pour over it 1 tablespoon browned butter mixed with ½ teaspoon wine vinegar. Rather special!

ONIONS   OMELETTE WITH YOUNG ONIONS
(Green onions, herbs)

Peel and slice 5 or 6 young onions together with part of their
green. The number used naturally will depend on their size.
Now cook them, stirring, in 1 or more tablespoons of butter
until soft and pale-gold. Season with salt and pepper and a
good pinch of sugar. Add 1 teaspoon finely chopped parsley.
Rub the bowl with a cut end of garlic before beating the eggs,
make your omelette, and fold the onions into the center.

ONIONS   ONION OMELETTE WITH APPLES
(Onion, apple, tomato, garlic)

Slice finely 1 onion and sauté in 1 tablespoon melted butter.
Add to this ½ an apple, cut in fine julienne strips. Allow to
soften together and add the flesh of 1 small tomato, peeled,
seeded, and diced, and 1 small mashed clove of garlic. Season
with salt and pepper and cook slowly until all moisture has
evaporated.
You should have about 4 tablespoons of this mixture to fold
into the center of a 6-egg omelette.

ONIONS   OMELETTE SOUBISE
(Onion, rice, stock)

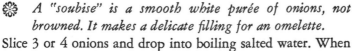 *A "soubise" is a smooth white purée of onions, not
browned. It makes a delicate filling for an omelette.*
Slice 3 or 4 onions and drop into boiling salted water. When
partly cooked, drain them and put them in a heavy saucepan
with 1 tablespoon of uncooked rice and enough chicken or

veal stock to cover. Cover the pan and braise on a very low fire for about 20 minutes to ½ an hour. Press through a fine sieve and if the resulting purée is not thick enough, return it to the fire and reduce to the desired consistency. Add a lump of fresh butter, and fold the purée soubise in the center of your omelette.

This omelette will be even finer if to your onion purée you add 1 cooked mashed chicken liver and 1 tablespoon of fried bread croutons.

PEAS   OMELETTE CLAMART
(Peas)

When you next cook small tender peas *à la française,* save about a cupful to use in an omelette. *Petits pois à la française* are small tender peas cooked slowly, in a heavy, covered saucepan, on a bed of shredded lettuce with 1 or 2 spring onions, a pinch of thyme, a sprig of parsley, a lump of butter, salt and pepper, and a little sugar. Add 2 or 3 tablespoons of water and braise slowly until tender and most of the liquid has evaporated, but the peas are still moist.

Reheat 1 cup of peas in a little butter. Put ¾ of the cup of peas in the center of the omelette before folding. After folding make a shallow slit on the top of the omelette and place the remaining peas in this.

PEAS   OMELETTE AU PETITS POIS PAUL REBOUX
(Peas, cream, egg yolk)

Paul Reboux, French gastronome, always ready with suggestions for gilding the lily, advises you to add 1 beaten egg yolk combined with 1 tablespoon of heavy cream to 1 cup of peas when heating them for an omelette filling. Season and heat carefully, stirring until slightly thickened. The same procedure may be followed with small amounts of leftover cooked vegetables such as carrots, *flageolets* or cooked dried beans, limas, string beans, sliced artichoke bottoms, *salsifis,* or almost any vegetable you can name. The result is indeed infinitely finer than mere "warmed over" vegetables.

PEPPERS   SWEET PEPPER OMELETTE
(Sweet peppers)

Remove the seeds from either a green or red sweet pepper, cut in rather small pieces, and sauté slowly in 1 tablespoon of butter until softened. Mix with the eggs before making the omelette.

PEPPERS   PIPERADE
(Sweet pepper, onion, garlic, tomatoes, ham)

❈ *This dish from the French Basque country is neither strictly an omelette nor strictly peppers. But as both eggs and sweet peppers enter into its manufacture it may as well go in here. It has a consistency somewhere between an omelette and scrambled eggs and makes an excellent simple luncheon dish.*

Slice a small sweet green pepper finely and sauté it very slowly in olive oil. Add salt and pepper, 1 small onion, chopped, 1 small clove of garlic, chopped and mashed, and 2 ripe tomatoes, peeled, seeded, and coarsely chopped. Add 1 generous tablespoon shredded cooked ham and simmer the mixture slowly for 20 to 30 minutes, or until the vegetables are soft. Add 1 tablespoon of butter.

Beat 4 eggs slightly with salt and pepper and stir them vigorously into the hot vegetable mixture, raising the heat so the eggs will cook quickly. This may be served directly from the pan.

POTATO   OMELETTE PARMENTIÈRE
(Potato, parsley)

Cut in small dice about ¾ cup of cooked potatoes and brown them on all sides in 1 tablespoon of butter. Just before making the omelette add to the eggs the potatoes and 1 generous teaspoon of finely chopped parsley. Serve flat or folded.
If you prefer, fold the potatoes and parsley into the center of the omelette when done.

POTATO   POTATO OMELETTE WITH ONION
(Potato, green onion)

Dice and brown in 1 tablespoon of butter ¾ cup of diced cooked potato. Add 1 or 2 scallions or 1 small spring onion, chopped, salt and pepper, and 1 teaspoon of parsley, chopped fine. When the onion is softened add the mixture to the eggs and make the omelette at once. Serve flat or folded.

POTATO   SAVOY POTATO OMELETTE (1)
(Potato, onion, cheese)

Sauté ¾ cup of diced cooked potato in 1 tablespoon of butter until crisp and brown on all sides. Chop 1 onion and cook this likewise in butter until soft and golden. Season potatoes and onion with salt and mix them with the eggs, together with 1 tablespoon of grated Swiss or Parmesan cheese, just before making the omelette.

POTATO   SAVOY POTATO OMELETTE (2)
(Potato, herbs, cheese)

Peel and slice 2 small potatoes in thin round slices and cook
them in butter until lightly browned on each side. Sprinkle
with salt and 1 teaspoon combined chervil and tarragon,
chopped. In beating the eggs, include, besides the seasonings,
1 generous tablespoon of Swiss cheese cut in very thin slivers
or chips. Make the omelette in the usual way, folding the
herb-flavored crisp potatoes into the center. The cheese will
punctuate the texture with tiny bits of creamy deliciousness.
Excellent!

POTATO   POTATO FRITTATA
(Potatoes, parsley, cinnamon)

Boil 3 average size potatoes, peel, and mash them to a purée.
Add 4 or 5 egg yolks, stir in well, and season with salt and
pepper. Add 2 egg whites, beaten stiff but not dry, 2 teaspoons
of finely chopped parsley, and a pinch of cinnamon. Mix all
well together.
Melt 1 tablespoon of butter in an omelette pan and spread in
the mixture evenly. Cook slowly until brown on one side, turn
carefully on a plate taking care not to break the omelette, add
more butter to the pan, and brown the other side.

POTATO, SWEET   SWEET POTATO OMELETTE
(Sweet potatoes, parsley)

This is made like the Omelette Parmentière, substituting sweet
potatoes for white ones.

Cut ¾ cup of cooked sweet potatoes in dice and brown them on all sides in 1 tablespoon of butter. They are softer than ordinary potatoes and may break up and not brown as evenly, but this is of little moment, as they can still be mingled with the 6 eggs, adding a good teaspoon of chopped parsley, and made into a delicious omelette, either flat or folded.

RICE   OMELETTE À L'INDIENNE
(Rice, stock, onion, cream, curry)

Sauté in 1 tablespoon of butter 1 small onion, chopped. When soft, add salt, 1 teaspoon of curry powder and cook for 2 minutes. Stir in 2 tablespoons of cream and add this mixture to the eggs before making the omelette.

When the omelette is cooked, fold into the center 1 cup of rice cooked as follows: wash thoroughly and dry on a towel ¼ cup of rice. Put into a saucepan with 1 tablespoon of melted butter and cook, stirring, until the rice is golden. Pour on about 1 cup of chicken stock, or enough to be completely absorbed when the rice is cooked. Cook slowly, and when the rice is cooked and the moisture evaporated, add a lump of butter.

Place the rice in the center of the omelette, fold it out and pour over the top ½ cup of cream sauce (see page 172.) flavored with a little curry. If you prefer to use leftover plain boiled rice, fry this in a little butter, adding 1 or 2 tablespoons of chicken stock for flavor.

SPINACH   OMELETTE AUX EPINARDS
(Spinach, chervil, cream sauce)

You may use leftover or fresh spinach for this omelette. In either case cook the spinach very briefly, chop it, and pass it through a fine strainer to make a purée. You will need about 4 tablespoons of the purée when cooked. Put it in a small saucepan, season, and add a lump of butter, a pinch of sugar, and a pinch of grated nutmeg. Stir it over the fire until all moisture has evaporated.

Add 1 teaspoon of chervil, chopped, and 1 tablespoon of the purée of spinach to the eggs before making the omelette. Fold the rest of the spinach into the center of the omelette and pour a few spoonfuls of cream sauce (see page 172) on top.

SPINACH   OMELETTE AUX EPINARDS,
                                PROVENÇALE

(Spinach, garlic, parsley)

Wash 3 or 4 handfuls of spinach, chop them coarsely, and squeeze out the water. Put them raw into a saucepan with 2 or 3 tablespoons of oil. Cook on a moderate fire, stirring, until softened and the juices have evaporated. Add salt, 1 small clove of garlic, chopped, and a good pinch of chopped parsley. Cook a few seconds more.

Add the spinach to your seasoned, beaten eggs and cook the omelette on both sides in oil instead of butter. To accomplish this turn it over whole onto a dish when done on one side, add a little more oil to the pan and, when hot, slide the omelette back off the dish to cook a few seconds on the other side. Slide out on a round platter and serve.

SPINACH   STUFFED FLORENTINE OMELETTE
(Spinach, Mornay sauce, cheese)

❀ *This omelette is something of a stunt, consisting of a*
     small spinach omelette, enclosed within a larger cheese

omelette. Quite a surprise to your guests and a good con-
versation piece! Make the smaller omelette in a small
pan, the larger one, of course, in a much larger pan to
enable the eggs to spread over a good area.

Make a small 3-egg omelette, mingling 2 or 3 tablespoons of
purée of spinach with the eggs before cooking. (The spinach
should be briefly cooked, drained of all water, chopped and
strained, and reheated in 1 tablespoon of browned butter with
a pinch each of salt, pepper, and grated nutmeg.) Keep this
little omelette warm while you make the large omelette, as
follows:

Beat 8 eggs as usual, with salt and pepper and 4 tablespoons
of grated Parmesan cheese. Cook in a good-sized pan in plenty
of butter, and when just done but still a little creamy on top,
place your little green omelette in the center and fold the
cheese omelette about it. This is quite a maneuver, but you
can do it. When perfectly placed and shaped in the center of
an oval ovenproof platter, pour ¾ cup of Mornay sauce (see
page 173) over the top. Sprinkle with a little more grated
cheese and place briefly under a very hot broiler to acquire
a golden tinge. Some would add a few tablespoons of tomato
sauce on each side of the omelette, but this beautiful dish is
really a thing of perfection without it.

SPINACH   FOAMY SPINACH OMELETTE
(Spinach, parsley, onion juice)

You will need about 1 cup of cooked spinach, finely chopped
and strained, and heated in a little butter until all moisture
has completely disappeared. Beat separately the yolks and
whites of 4 eggs until the yolks are thick and the whites are
stiff. Mix the spinach into the yolks together with salt and
pepper, 1 teaspoon of parsley, chopped, and 1 tablespoon of

onion juice. Fold in the egg whites and mix well. Melt 3 tablespoons of butter in an omelette pan, put in the omelette mixture, and cook over a slow fire. When almost done, you may place it under a hot broiler for a few seconds to finish cooking. Or simply fold out double on the platter if you prefer your omelette rather creamy.

SPINACH   GERMAN OMELETTE WITH SPINACH
(Creamed spinach)

Make 2 thin German omelettes according to the basic recipe (see page 22) and before rolling them up, spread with spinach purée made as follows: heat 1½ cups of finely chopped or strained cooked spinach in 1 tablespoon of butter. Add a pinch of nutmeg and sprinkle with 1 teaspoon of flour. Blend and add ¼ cup of heavy cream, or stock. Heat and stir until thickened. Spread on the omelettes, roll them up, cut in sections, and serve with roast meat.

SQUASH   OMELETTE AUX COURGETTES
(Summer squash, parsley)

Italian zucchini are best for this omelette, although other small summer squash may be used. You may make this omelette in the pan in which the squash are first cooked, mingling together over the fire and serving it in the pan, or you may cook the vegetable first, combine it with the beaten eggs in the bowl, pour all into the omelette pan, and fold out in the usual form.
Cut 1 or 2 zucchini into thin slices and sauté them slowly in 2 tablespoons of butter until soft and all liquid has evaporated. The quantity should make ¾ cup to 1 cup when

cooked. Season with salt and pepper. Pour in your beaten, seasoned eggs to which you have added 1 tablespoon parsley, chopped. Stir all together with a fork and when set, serve directly from the pan.

If you plan to mix the cooked squash with the eggs before making the omelette, a procedure less likely to make it stick to the pan, cut the squash in small dice before cooking.

SQUASH   ITALIAN OVEN OMELETTE
(Zucchini, bread crumbs, cheese, lemon rind)

Mix together 1 medium-sized zucchini (Italian squash) cut into dice, 1 tablespoon of bread crumbs soaked in ½ cup of milk, 1 tablespoon grated Parmesan cheese, ½ teaspoon grated lemon rind, a good pinch of salt, and a pinch of sugar. Stir the mixture into 6 beaten eggs and pour into a shallow baking dish which has first been greased with olive oil and sprinkled with bread crumbs. Cook about 20 minutes in a hot (400°) oven.

SQUASH (BLOSSOMS)   SQUASH-BLOSSOM OMELETTE
(Squash flowers, tomato sauce)

✿ *The flowers of the squash vine are used in Southern France to make an excellent omelette. The next time you have some to spare from your own garden try it for yourself.*

Cut up the petals of the flowers coarsely, rejecting the center. Cook these gently in butter or oil until tender. Season with salt and pepper and mix them with the eggs, beaten lightly with salt and pepper and a teaspoon of chopped parsley. Make

the omelette in the usual way and when it is folded out on the
platter, surround it with a small stream of thick tomato sauce.

✿ *It would seem that many other omelettes in this collec-
tion might be included in the general category of tomato
omelettes, notably some under the heading of "Mixed
Vegetables," like the Spanish Omelettes. But whereas
tomatoes or tomato sauce are called for to add savor to
many a combination, in the ones presently considered
the tomato may definitely be said to predominate. As the
acid of fresh tomatoes when combined with raw eggs
may tend to make them separate in the cooking, it is
usually better to use them as a filling for the already
cooked omelette.*

TOMATO   TOMATO OMELETTE WITH HERBS
(Tomato, herbs)

Peel 2 medium-sized tomatoes, cut in half, remove seeds, and
dice the pulp. Cook them until soft in 1 generous tablespoon
of butter together with salt and pepper, a pinch of cinnamon
or nutmeg, 1 teaspoon parsley, chopped, ¼ teaspoon of marjoram or tarragon, chopped. Either of these herbs adds a
delicious flavor to the mixture. When softened, fold into the
center of a 6-egg omelette.

TOMATO   TOMATO OMELETTE PROVENÇALE
(Tomato, onion, garlic, parsley)

Peel, seed, and dice 2 tomatoes and cook them in 2 or 3 tablespoons of oil with 2 slices of onion, chopped, until soft and

the liquid has evaporated. Add salt and pepper, one clove of
garlic, chopped and mashed, and 1 tablespoon of parsley,
chopped. Simmer 1 minute and fold into the center of a 6-egg
omelette.

TOMATO   TOMATO OMELETTE NIÇOISE
(Tomato, garlic, parsley, anchovies)

Peel, seed, and dice 2 tomatoes and cook them until soft in 1
tablespoon of oil combined with 1 tablespoon of butter. Add
salt and pepper, 1 clove of garlic, chopped and mashed, and
1 tablespoon of chopped parsley. Pour 6 beaten, seasoned
eggs into 1 tablespoon melted butter in the omelette pan and
add the tomatoes to them immediately, stirring to mix the ingredients well. When sufficiently cooked on the bottom, place
for a few seconds under a hot broiler to finish cooking the top.
Slide out flat onto the platter, lay a few anchovy filets diago-
nally or in lozenge design on top, pour over 2 tablespoons of
browned butter, and serve.

TOMATO   OMELETTE À L'ÉCARLATE
(Tomatoes, onion, herbs, mushrooms, ham, stock)

Sauté 2 onions, chopped, in 3 or 4 tablespoons of oil. When
soft and slightly browned, add 4 or 5 tomatoes, chopped, ¼
teaspoon of thyme, ½ a bay leaf, salt, 3 or 4 bruised pepper-
corns, 2 or 3 mushrooms, chopped (or the equivalent amount
in mushroom stems), 1 tablespoon of scraps of lean ham, and
½ cup of consommé or stock. Simmer all together for about
½ hour. Force this sauce through a fine sieve. Reduce over the
fire until quite thick, adding ½ teaspoon of meat glaze or
extract. Stir 2 tablespoons of this purée into the eggs when

making the omelette. When folded out on the platter spread
the rest of the tomato mixture on top.

TOMATO   TOMATO AND BACON OMELETTE
(Tomato, bacon, shallot)

Peel and slice, in rather thick slices, 2 large firm tomatoes.
Sauté these slices in 2 tablespoons of butter about 2 minutes
on each side. Season with salt and pepper. In another pan
brown 2 generous tablespoons of diced lean bacon, adding 1
shallot, chopped, for the last minutes of cooking.
Place the slices of tomato carefully in a row in the center of
a 6-egg omelette, drain out the bacon cubes from the fat, and
arrange them on top of the tomatoes. Fold the omelette and
serve.

TRUFFLE   OMELETTE AUX TRUFFES
(Truffles, Madeira sauce)

❈ *This omelette is fairly common in the French province
of Périgord, homeland of the truffle. For us it is a rarer
luxury. A small can of truffles usually contains 2, sometimes 3, truffles.*
When beating the eggs for your omelette, add 1 diced truffle
which has been just barely heated in a little butter. After the
omelette has been folded out, place a row of round slices of
truffle, likewise heated in butter, along the top. Over these
pour 2 or 3 tablespoons of sauce made as follows: combine
the juices from the can of truffles with ½ teaspoon of meat
glaze or extract, blend with ½ teaspoon of potato starch and
2 tablespoons of water. Simmer together for 1 or 2 minutes,
add 1 teaspoon of Madeira, reheat, taste for seasoning.

TRUFFLE   OMELETTE CAVALIÈRE
(Truffles, Madeira, cream)

❀ *This is a veritable delicacy.*
Slice 2 or 3 truffles (the contents of a small can) and warm
them a few seconds in 1 generous teaspoon of butter, reserving the juices from the can. Sprinkle them with ½ teaspoon
of flour, blend, and stir in the juices. Now add 1 tablespoon of
Madeira, 3 tablespoons of heavy cream, and ¼ teaspoon of
meat glaze or extract. Season, simmer until slightly thickened,
and fold into the center of a 6-egg omelette.

WATERCRESS   WATERCRESS OMELETTE
(Watercress)

Chop coarsely enough watercress to make 1 cup. Make a
6-egg omelette and as soon as it begins to take on consistency,
sprinkle on the watercress and stir it a little into the eggs.
Finish cooking, fold out, and serve, garnished with more watercress if desired.

SWEET DESSERT
OMELETTES

SWEET DESSERT
OMELETTES

Sweet omelettes range from the very simple fresh fruit types, containing a minimum of sugar, to the more elaborate mousseline and soufflé omelettes, and those served with whipped cream or a sauce; or the dressiest of all, the Norvégienne (or Surprise). This is a more delicious form of Baked Alaska, as the top contains yolks as well as whites, and the resulting meringue is creamy and delicious. The simple fruit recipes will please those who find elaborate desserts too rich and cloying, and the others will be the delight of true dessert lovers. It is wise to keep a special jar of granulated sugar with a long vanilla bean sunk through its depths for use in making desserts. When "vanilla-flavored sugar" is mentioned, this is what is indicated. Although, of course, sugar and a little vanilla extract will do.

In the days of coal stoves the sugar coating of a dessert omelette was caramelized with a red-hot poker in criss-cross pattern along the top. This may still be done with gas if you have a suitable thin iron instrument, and the result is decorative as well as delicious. But for purposes of convenience you are advised in the following recipes to brown the sugar briefly under a very hot broiler.

Where grated rind, or "zest," of orange or lemon peel is mentioned, this indicates only the outer or colored part, not including the white pulp.

In any omelette where yolks and whites of egg are beaten separately a hand electric beater is useful. The yolks should be whipped very thoroughly until pale and as thick as possible. You are warned not to overdo the beating of the whites. They should be whipped until stiff but not dry, which means just to the point where they stand up in creamy peaks as you lift out the beater. The cooked result should be creamy and not dry.

ALMOND   ALMOND SOUFFLÉ OMELETTE

Use the basic recipe for soufflé omelette (see page 24), replacing the vanilla by 1 teaspoon of almond extract and 3 tablespoons of chopped almonds.

ALMOND AND APPLE   ALMOND OMELETTE À LA
REINE PÉDAUQUE

(Apple, cream, meringue, almond flavoring)

For this dessert omelette in layers, mix 3 eggs with 1 tablespoon of heavy cream, a pinch of salt, and 1 teaspoon of powdered almond or a few drops of almond extract. The second omelette is made in identical proportions, but it is best to mix them separately. Make a thick applesauce by stewing 3 peeled, quartered apples in 3 tablespoons butter with 3 tablespoons sugar. When soft, strain them and reduce until quite thick, blending in 2 or 3 tablespoons of heavy cream and 1 teaspoon of kirsch. Make the first omelette in 1 tablespoon of hot butter, and slide it, without folding, onto a round ovenproof dish.
Spread the apple mixture on the first omelette and place the second omelette on top. Cover with a meringue of 2 stiffly beaten egg whites mixed with 2 tablespoons granulated sugar

and a few drops of almond extract. Sprinkle with sugar and brown quickly in a very hot oven.

APPLE   OMELETTE NORMANDE
(Apple, apple brandy)

❀ *The French province famous for its apples and apple brandy lends its name to this simple and excellent dessert.*

Peel and chop coarsely 3 firm cooking apples. Cook slowly in 1½ tablespoons of butter with 1½ tablespoons of vanilla-flavored granulated sugar. When soft, add 1 tablespoon of apple brandy. Add 2 tablespoons of sugar to 6 eggs when beating them for the omelette. Fill the omelette with the apple mixture, fold out, sprinkle with sugar, and glaze under a hot broiler. Send to the table flaming with 2 tablespoons of warmed apple brandy. Cream may be served with this if desired.

APPLE   PLAIN APPLE OMELETTE
(Apples)

Core and peel 2 whole apples. Cut them in thin round slices and sauté gently over a low fire, on both sides, in 2 tablespoons of butter, till cooked, keeping the slices whole. Make a 6-egg omelette containing 2 tablespoons of sugar and place the apples neatly over the surface of the omelette immediately after pouring the eggs into the pan. Sprinkle generously with sugar, allow the eggs to finish cooking slowly and rather thoroughly, and serve flat.

APPLE   APPLE OMELETTE BLANDIN
(Apples, rum)

Peel, core, and quarter 2 apples. Cut them in very thin slices and sprinkle over them 1 tablespoon of rum and 2 tablespoons of sugar. To make this omelette blend 4 tablespoons of flour, ½ cup of milk, and a pinch of salt. Add the beaten yolks of 2 eggs and when quite smoothly blended, fold in the 2 whites beaten stiff but not dry. Mix in the apples with care. Melt 1 generous tablespoon of butter in the omelette pan and make an omelette with half of this mixture. Turn it to cook the other side. Make a second like the first and serve them flat and well sprinkled with sugar.

In the same way you may make omelettes of cherries, apricots, peaches, etc.

APPLE AND APRICOT   MERINGUE OMELETTE
(Apples, apricot jam, orange rind)

Beat 2 egg whites until stiff to make a light meringue, adding 2 tablespoons of sugar.

Make a 4-egg omelette adding the grated rind of an orange to the eggs. Place the omelette flat on a round platter and spread it with apple-apricot filling made as follows:

Peel and core 2 apples, chop them coarsely, and cook them till soft in 2 tablespoons of butter and 2 tablespoons of sugar. Mash them to a purée and cook out any surplus juice. Stir in 2 tablespoons of strained apricot jam.

When the fruit is spread on the omelette, cover it with the meringue and place in a very hot oven until the meringue is lightly browned. If you desire to make this omelette even more handsome, press some of the meringue through a paper cornucopia to form rosettes and place a bit of red currant jelly in the center of each.

APRICOT   CÉLESTINE OMELETTE
(Apricot jam)

❀ *This is a series of 1- or 2-egg omelettes, depending on your taste, filled with apricot jam, glazed with sugar, and arranged in a decorative mound.*

Break 10 eggs into a bowl, add 1 teaspoon of salt, 3 table-spoons of sugar, and 3 tablespoons of water. Beat moderately as for a plain omelette. Melt 1 teaspoon of butter in a small omelette pan and pour in, with the aid of a small ladle, a quantity equal to 2 eggs. The omelette should be rather thin. Turn and cook very briefly on the other side. Slide onto a greased cookie sheet. Continue in this way until you have used all the eggs, adding butter to the pan before making each omelette. Spread each one with strained apricot jam, or well sweetened, thick, stewed apricots passed through a strainer. Roll each one up separately, sprinkle each with sugar, and glaze briefly under the broiler. Arrange in layers or a pyramid on a platter and serve.

APRICOT   RUM APRICOT OMELETTE
(Apricot jam, whipped cream)

Fill a 6-egg omelette with warmed apricot jam before folding out on the platter. Sprinkle the top with sugar, pour on several tablespoons of slightly warmed rum, and set aflame just before serving. Pass in a separate sauce dish cold whipped cream, flavored with sugar and a few drops of almond extract, to complete this delectable dessert.

APRICOT   APRICOT OMELETTES FLAMBÉES
(Apricot jam, cream, orange rind, liqueurs)

Beat 3 eggs lightly with 1 tablespoon of heavy cream, 2 tablespoons of cold water, a small pinch of salt, and 1 teaspoon of
sugar. With this make 4 thin omelettes in a small omelette
pan and spread them on a board or baking sheet to cool.

Take 5 to 6 tablespoons of strained apricot jam, or well
sweetened, cold stewed and strained apricots which have been
cooked to a thick consistency. Mix them with 2 tablespoons of
whipped cream. Place 2 tablespoons of the mixture in the
center of each omelette, roll them up, place them side by side
on an oval dish, and sprinkle with a little orange juice and
grated zest of orange rind.

Now sprinkle lavishly with sugar, pour over ½ a liqueur
glass of rum, the same amount of kirsch, and set aflame. Serve,
spooning the flaming liquid continually over the omelettes
until the fire dies.

BANANA   BANANA OMELETTE
(Bananas)

Make a sugar syrup by boiling ½ cup of vanilla-flavored
sugar with 1 cup of water until clear. Peel and slice 2 ripe
bananas and simmer them in the syrup until tender. Drain
them from the syrup and place in the center of a 6-egg omelette before folding out on an ovenproof platter. Pour the remaining syrup over the omelette, sprinkle with granulated
sugar, and glaze under a hot broiler.

CANDIED FRUITS   OMELETTE GEORGE SAND
(Candied fruits, frangipane cream)

Add 2 tablespoons of sugar and a pinch of salt to 6 eggs when beating them for an omelette. When almost cooked, spread over the omelette 3 tablespoons of candied fruits cut in small pieces. (Orange, lemon, pineapple, cherries, etc.) Fold once and slide onto the platter. Over the surface spread a layer of frangipane (or pastry cream) (see Frangipane Omelette, page 143). Sprinkle this evenly with sugar and glaze briefly under a hot broiler. Decorate the surface with pieces of candied fruits in a pretty pattern and surround with *marrons glacés* (candied chestnuts), or marrons in syrup.

CHERRIES   CHERRY OMELETTE
(Cherries)

Remove the stems and pits from about 30 cherries and cook them in butter until slightly softened. Add the cherries to the 6 sweetened eggs, beaten for an omelette. Make the omelette flat rather than folded. Slide it out on a round platter, sprinkle lavishly with sugar, pour over several tablespoons of warmed rum, which you set aflame at the moment of serving.

CHESTNUTS   OMELETTE AUX MARRONS GLACÉS
(Candied chestnuts, kirsch)

Make a sweet mousseline omelette (see page 149) and, at the moment of folding, spread in the center several tablespoons of crumbled *marrons glacés* (candied chestnuts) which have been sprinkled with 1 tablespoon of kirsch. Sprinkle the omelette with sugar, glaze quickly under a hot broiler, and set aflame with several tablespoons of kirsch at the moment of serving.

CHOCOLATE　　CHOCOLATE OMELETTE MOUSSELINE
(Chocolate)

Melt 1 ounce of semi-sweet chocolate with 1 tablespoon of water over gentle heat. Allow to cool. Stir in 4 very well beaten egg yolks, 5 tablespoons of sugar, and a pinch of salt. Beat the 4 whites until stiff and mix all together. Melt 2 generous tablespoons of butter in an omelette pan, pour in the mixture, and cook over a moderate flame, stirring the outer edges toward the center, until cooked, but not dry. Fold out double and serve with chocolate sauce (see page 172).

CHOCOLATE　　CHOCOLATE CREAM OMELETTE
(Chocolate, milk, cornstarch, ladyfingers)

Melt 2 ounces of sweet chocolate with 2 tablespoons of milk in the top of a double boiler. Add gradually 1½ cups of milk and stir until it comes to a boil. Blend 2 tablespoons of rice flour or cornstarch with 2 tablespoons of milk, and when smooth, add it to the chocolate, stirring with a sauce whisk. Allow to simmer gently in the double boiler for 15 minutes, but do not boil.
Make a 6-egg omelette, sweetened with 2 tablespoons of sugar, and fold half of the chocolate cream in the center. When folded out on the platter, place halves of ladyfingers about it and decorate the ladyfingers and the top of the omelette with the remaining chocolate cream by means of a pastry bag. Sprinkle a little sugar on the surfaces and glaze briefly under a hot broiler.

CHOCOLATE   CHOCOLATE SOUFFLÉ OMELETTE

Melt 1½ ounces of semi-sweet chocolate with 1 tablespoon of
water over gentle heat. Allow to cool. Beat 4 egg yolks with
½ cup of granulated sugar long and thoroughly until thick
and pale. Add the chocolate. Fold in the stiffly beaten whites
of 6 eggs and continue according to recipe for soufflé omelette
(see page 24). Serve with chocolate sauce (see page 172).

COFFEE   COFFEE SOUFFLÉ OMELETTE

Use the basic recipe for soufflé omelette (see page 24), replacing the vanilla by 3 tablespoons of very strong coffee.

COFFEE   COFFEE AND ALMOND SOUFFLÉ
                                      OMELETTE
(Coffee, almonds)

Beat the yolks of 4 eggs with 6 tablespoons of sugar long and
thoroughly until thick and pale. Add 3 tablespoons of extremely strong coffee. Fold in 6 whites beaten stiff and ½
cup grilled chopped almonds (unsalted). Drop the mixture
into a buttered oval baking dish, smooth the surface with a
spatula, leaving it higher in the center.
Place in a hot oven and when the omelette begins to rise
(which should be in about 5 minutes), make a long slit in
the surface, and continue to cook about 10 minutes more.

FRANGIPANE   SMALL OMELETTES FRANGIPANE
(Pastry cream with macaroons)

❀ *This is a real party dessert. The cream filling can be
prepared ahead of time and the omelettes completed
just before serving.*

This is a series of small 1- or 2-egg omelettes made separately in your smallest pan and filled with a delectable cream filling called frangipane.

Beat a number of eggs equivalent to the number of little omelettes you wish to serve. For 10 eggs add 3 tablespoons of sugar, 2 tablespoons of melted butter, a pinch of salt, and ½ cup of cream. Make 10 small omelettes separately, adding butter to the little pan each time and spreading the omelettes flat on baking sheets or a board as completed. Spread a layer of frangipane filling on each, roll them up, sprinkle with sugar, and glaze under the broiler. Arrange in a mound on the platter and serve.

Frangipane Filling (or Pastry Cream)

In a saucepan mix ½ cup of sugar, ½ cup of sifted flour, and ⅛ teaspoon of salt. Stir in 1 whole egg and 2 egg yolks, slightly beaten. Work thoroughly together. Add gradually 1½ cups of scalded milk and 1 teaspoon of vanilla. Heat over the fire, stirring continually, until it begins to cook. Cook for 3 minutes, stirring. Remove to a bowl, cool a little, and work in 2 tablespoons of butter and 4 tablespoons dried, rolled macaroon crumbs. Instead of macaroons you may flavor this cream with lemon or almond extract, rum or brandy. In this case it is called pastry cream. The name frangipane is given to it where it contains macaroons.

JAM   JAM OMELETTE
(Jam, lemon rind, rum)

For a 6-egg omelette add 2 tablespoons of sugar and a small pinch of salt. Grated lemon rind may be added also if you desire. Make the omelette in the usual way and fill it with apricot, strawberry, peach, or raspberry jam, or any other jam which pleases you. When folded out, sprinkle with sugar and glaze under the broiler. Two tablespoons of warmed rum or brandy flamed over the top at the last minute perfects the flavor.

JAM JAM OMELETTE WITH FRUIT

Make as the jam omelette, filling with sliced preserved, or stewed, fruit combined with jam. Sliced apples with currant jelly, diced pineapple with apricot jam, sliced peaches or pears with raspberry jelly are all delicious fillings for this omelette.

JAM CHERRY JAM OMELETTE WITH KIRSCH
(Cherry jam, kirsch)

Prepare 6 eggs for an omelette, seasoned with a small pinch of salt and 2 tablespoons of sugar. Fill it with cherry jam before folding out on the platter. Sprinkle with sugar, glaze it under the broiler, and set aflame with 2 or 3 tablespoons of kirsch at the moment of serving.

JELLY SWEET GERMAN OMELETTES
(Jelly or jam)

Make 2 thin German omelettes according to the basic recipe (see page 22). Spread each one with currant jelly, strawberry jam, or any other jelly or jam of your choice, before rolling up. Sprinkle lavishly with sugar and serve.

JELLY CURRANT JELLY OMELETTE
(Currant jelly, raspberry sauce)

Add 2 tablespoons of sugar to a 6-egg omelette and fill it with 3 or 4 tablespoons of currant jelly. Sprinkle with sugar

and glaze briefly under a hot broiler, if desired. Pour a trickle
of raspberry syrup, or Melba sauce, along the top and serve.

LEMON   LEMON SOUFFLÉ OMELETTE

Use the basic recipe for soufflé omelette (see page 24), replacing the vanilla by the juice and grated rind of 1 lemon.

LEMON   LEMON GERMAN OMELETTE
(Lemon rind and juice)

Add the grated rind and juice of 1 lemon and 3 tablespoons of
sugar to the batter for German omelettes (see page 22) before cooking. Sprinkle with sugar and serve.

LIQUEUR   CURAÇAO OMELETTE
(Curaçao and brandy)

Make a plain omelette, taking care not to overcook it, and
when folded out on the platter, cut a series of shallow slashes
across the top from side to side. Pour over 2 tablespoons of
curaçao and 2 tablespoons of brandy and sprinkle with sugar.
Set aflame and serve. The same omelette may be made with
kirsch, apple brandy, any other fruit liqueur, rum, or whisky.

LIQUEUR   RUM OMELETTE MOUSSELINE
(Lemon rind, rum)

Beat 4 egg yolks long and thoroughly, until pale and thick,
with the grated zest of 1 lemon, 2 tablespoons of cream, 6

tablespoons of sugar, and ⅛ teaspoon of salt. Beat the whites until stiff but not dry and combine with the yolks. Cook the omelette in 2½ tablespoons of butter and turn out while still very creamy, taking great care not to overcook it. Sprinkle with sugar and caramelize quickly under a hot broiler. Pour over 4 tablespoons of warmed rum and set aflame.

LIQUEUR   RUM SOUFFLÉ OMELETTE

Use the basic recipe for soufflé omelette (see page 24), replacing the vanilla by 2 tablespoons of rum, kirsch, or other liqueurs.

MACAROONS   MACAROON OMELETTE
(Macaroons, almond extract)

To 6 beaten eggs add 3 dried macaroons rolled into crumbs, 1½ tablespoons of granulated sugar, a small pinch of salt, and a few drops of almond extract. Make the omelette in the usual way.

MACAROONS   DIJON OMELETTE
(Macaroons, pastry cream, black currant syrup, meringue)

Roll 3 dried macaroons into crumbs, add half the crumbs together with 1 scant tablespoon of sugar to 3 eggs, and make a flat omelette which you slide out onto a round platter. Repeat the process for a second identical omelette. Cover the first omelette with a layer of pastry cream (see Small Omelettes Frangipane, page 143) flavored with almond extract and a little *cassis* (black currant) syrup. Place the second omelette on top and cover with a meringue of 2 egg whites beaten with a little sugar. Sprinkle sugar on the top and brown delicately in a very hot oven. Pour a little *cassis* syrup around the omelette and serve.

MACAROON   CREAM MACAROON OMELETTE
(Macaroons, apple jelly, cream)

Roll 3 large, dried macaroons into crumbs and add 3 tablespoons of apple jelly and 1 tablespoon of whipped cream. This constitutes the filling for a 6-egg omelette. When turned out on the platter, sprinkle with sugar and glaze under the broiler. Serve with whipped cream.

MACAROON   SOUFFLÉ MACAROON OMELETTE
(Macaroons)

Beat 4 egg yolks very thoroughly with ½ cup of granulated sugar until light in color and quite thick. Beat 6 whites until stiff but not dry and fold them carefully into the yolks together with 6 dried macaroons rolled into fine crumbs. Pour into a generously buttered shallow oval baking dish, slash along the top, and cook in a moderately hot oven (350°) until lightly golden on top, still creamy inside. A few minutes before it is done sprinkle with sifted sugar.

MINCEMEAT   CHRISTMAS OMELETTE
(Orange rind, mincemeat, rum)

✾ *This is a delicious and less heavy substitute for mince pie, and it is of course far easier and quicker to make.*
Add to 6 eggs, when beating them, the grated rind of 1 orange, 2 tablespoons of sugar, and 1 tablespoon of rum. Fill

the center of the omelette with warmed mincemeat before folding out. Sprinkle with sugar and flame with 3 tablespoons of warmed rum at the moment of serving.

MOUSSELINE   SWEET MOUSSELINE OMELETTE

Separate the yolks and whites of 4 eggs. Beat the yolks very thoroughly with 6 tablespoons of sugar and a few drops of vanilla. Beat the whites until stiff but not dry and combine rather thoroughly with the yolks. Cook in 2 generous table-spoons of butter, slowly and with care, as the sugar is inclined to stick. Turn double, slide out on a platter, and sprinkle with sugar. Never overcook a mousseline omelette.

NORVÉGIENNE (OR SURPRISE)   OMELETTE À LA
NORVÉGIENNE or OMELETTE SURPRISE
(Sponge cake, ice cream, meringue with yolks)

❀ *Rumor has it that the Surprise omelette was invented by Benjamin Thompson, Count Rumford of Massachusetts, perhaps to demonstrate the wonders of the Rumford oven which he invented.*

This exquisite dish resembles the Baked Alaska and is a fitting end for the finest banquet. The following recipe will serve 12. It can be made on one large oval board or two separate plates. Make a ¾-inch layer of *genoise,* or sponge cake, that will fit the board on which the omelette is to be made and served. (If you prefer, bake your cake in 2 round layer-cake pans to cover 2 large round plates.) Sprinkle the cake with kirsch, or rum, and cover with a flattened mound of ice cream, leaving a half-inch border of cake around the edge. Cover with a thick layer of soufflé omelette mixture (see below) decorated with a pastry tube, or simply smoothed with a spatula. Sprinkle with sifted confectioner's sugar and brown quickly in a very hot oven (450°–500°) for about 5 minutes, or until lightly browned.

Soufflé Omelette Mixture—Beat 4 egg yolks with 1 generous cup of sugar until thick and pale in color. Flavor with almond or vanilla extract, or a liqueur, and fold in very delicately 10 stiffly beaten egg whites.

ORANGE   ORANGE OMELETTE MOUSSELINE
(Orange rind and juices, curaçao)

Separate the yolks and whites of 4 eggs. Beat the yolks thoroughly, together with the grated outer rind of 1 orange, 3 tablespoons of orange juice, 1 teaspoon of flour, and 6 tablespoons of sugar. Beat the whites until stiff and combine the two. Make the omelette in the usual way, in 2 generous tablespoons of butter. Turn double and slide out on a platter. Sprinkle with sugar and 3 tablespoons of curaçao.

The grated outer rind of 1 lemon and 2 tablespoons of lemon juice may be used in place of orange.

ORANGE   ORANGE SOUFFLÉ OMELETTE

Use the basic recipe for soufflé omelette (see page 24), replacing the vanilla by 3 tablespoons of the juice and the grated rind of 1 orange.

PINEAPPLE   OMELETTE BOURBONNAISE
(Pineapple, lemon rind, apricot jam, rum)

Beat 6 eggs with 2 tablespoons of sugar, a small pinch of salt, and the grated zest of 1 lemon rind. Before folding out, fill it with 2 tablespoons finely diced fresh or canned pineapple combined with 2 tablespoons strained apricot jam. Fold on the platter, sprinkle with sugar, and pour over 3 tablespoons of warmed rum which is set aflame at the moment of serving.

PINEAPPLE   **PINEAPPLE OMELETTE**
(Pineapple slices)

❀ *Until you have tasted hot, fresh pineapple you will not realize how this treatment enhances the flavor of this and many other fruits.*

Boil ¾ cup of water with ¾ cup of vanilla-flavored sugar for 5 minutes. In this syrup simmer 4 thin slices of fresh pineapple until tender (about 12 minutes). Cut half the pineapple in small dice and mix them with the eggs when preparing a plain omelette. When it is turned out on the platter, sprinkle it with sugar, glaze it briefly under a hot broiler, and surround it with the rest of the pineapple cut in quarters. Pour the remaining hot syrup over the top.

PUMPKIN   **PUMPKIN OMELETTE**
(Pumpkin, spices)

Heat several tablespoons of cooked mashed pumpkin with a lump of butter, 1 tablespoon of sugar, and a pinch each of cinnamon, clove, and nutmeg. Beat it well and thin it with a little cream if necessary. This may be folded into the center of the omelette or beaten with the eggs when preparing the omelette. Sprinkle the omelette with sugar before folding and again on the surface when folded on the platter. Glaze under a hot broiler.

RAISINS   CORINTHIAN OMELETTE
(Raisins, pistachio nuts)

Beat 6 eggs with 1 tablespoon of rum, 2 tablespoons of sugar, and a small pinch of salt. Add ½ cup of soft raisins together with about 2 dozen shelled pistachio nuts cut in slivers. Make the omelette in the usual way, sprinkle with sugar, and glaze briefly under a hot broiler.

RASPBERRY   MELBA OMELETTE
(Raspberry jam, kirsch)

Place in a small saucepan 4 tablespoons of raspberry jam and stir in 1 tablespoon of kirsch and 1 tablespoon of prunelle or other fruit liqueur. Heat and stir for 2 minutes and pour this over the surface of a 6-egg omelette when folded out on the platter.

STRAWBERRY   SOUFFLÉ OMELETTE WITH
                                             STRAWBERRIES
(Strawberries, kirsch)

Cover the bottom of an oval shallow baking dish with 2 cups fresh strawberries which have been halved and sprinkled with ¼ cup of sugar and 2 tablespoons of kirsch or rum. Cover with the mixture for a sweet soufflé omelette and cook in the oven in the usual way. The same may be done with fresh raspberries or any fine jam.

STRAWBERRY   STRAWBERRY OMELETTE
(Strawberries, rum, cream)

Soak 1 cup of strawberries, cut in quarters, with ½ cup of
sugar, a few drops of lemon juice, and 2 tablespoons of kirsch
or rum. Keep in the refrigerator 1 hour before using. Add 2
tablespoons of sugar to 6 eggs for making your omelette.
When ready to make the omelette, drain the berries from the
juices, reserving the latter. Mix the cold berries with 2 tablespoons of whipped cream and fold into the center of your hot
omelette. Pour the remaining juices along the side of the
platter and serve immediately. This omelette is also delicious
without the added cream.

WALNUTS   WALNUT OMELETTE MOUSSELINE
(Walnuts, bread crumbs)

Soak 1 cup of walnut meats in salted cold water until the
skins soften a little. Drain and peel them, dry them on a
cloth, and chop them finely.
Soak ½ cup of soft bread crumbs in ½ cup sweetened water
and mix thoroughly with 4 well-beaten egg yolks. Beat the
whites until stiff and blend with the yolks.
Cook in 2 generous tablespoons of butter and when partly
cooked stir in the walnuts. Finish cooking, fold over once, and
slide out on a platter.

MISCELLANEOUS
OMELETTES & SAUCES

MISCELLANEOUS OMELETTES

BAKED   RUSSIAN BATTER OMELETTE
(Cream, flour, eggs, butter)

Blend gradually 1 cup of cream into ¾ cup of flour until
smooth. Add salt and pepper, then 6 eggs, one by one, stirring
after each addition. Beat well. Melt ¼ pound of butter in an
omelette pan. Pour in the batter and bake in a hot oven
(400°). When done, slide onto a round platter and pour
over the excess butter which should be browned.

BREAD CROUTONS   OMELETTE AUX CROUTONS
(Bread croutons, parsley)

Sauté 3 tablespoons of diced bread in 1 tablespoon of butter
over a gentle heat, stirring occasionally, until browned on all
sides. Combine these bread croutons, together with 1 teaspoon
of parsley, chopped, with 6 eggs beaten for an omelette.
Make the omelette in the usual way and turn out on a platter.

BREAD CRUMBS   BREAD-CRUMB FRITTATA
(Bread crumbs, butter, cream)

Sauté 3 tablespoons of white bread crumbs in 1 tablespoon of
melted butter until slightly browned. Stir in 2 tablespoons of

cream and add this mixture to 6 eggs slightly beaten, with a
pinch each of salt and pepper. Melt 2 tablespoons of butter
in your hot omelette pan and pour in the mixture. Stir once
or twice, and when set and slightly browned on the bottom,
turn and brown on the other side. Or, if you prefer, brown the
top quickly under a hot broiler. Slide out flat on a round
platter and serve at once.

BREAD CRUMBS   MOUSSELINE OMELETTE À LA
                                         POLONAISE
(Bread crumbs)

Make a mousseline omelette of 4 eggs and turn it out on a
platter. In a saucepan heat ⅛ pound of butter (4 tablespoons) and when it begins to foam up, drop in ¾ cup of
coarse bread crumbs. Stir and when the crumbs have browned
a little, pour the contents of the saucepan over the omelette.

CAPERS   OMELETTE WITH CAPERS
(Capers, parsley)

Add 2 tablespoons of capers and 1 teaspoon of finely chopped
parsley to 6 eggs beaten for an omelette. Cook and fold out
in the usual way.

CHEESE   CHEESE OMELETTE (1)
(Swiss and Parmesan cheese)

Add 1½ tablespoons of grated Gruyère (Swiss) cheese and
1½ tablespoons of grated Parmesan to 6 eggs beaten for an

omelette. Add a good pinch of pepper and only a small pinch of salt as the cheese supplies a salty flavor also. Make the omelette in the usual way. You may sprinkle a small amount of grated cheese on the surface of the folded omelette if desired.

CHEESE   CHEESE OMELETTE (2)
(Cheese, tomato sauce)

Add 1½ tablespoons of grated Parmesan to 6 beaten eggs together with a good pinch of pepper and a very small pinch of salt. When the omelette is partly cooked, sprinkle 1½ tablespoons of diced Gruyère over the surface. Complete the cooking, fold out on a platter, and surround with tomato sauce (see page 175).

CHEESE   CHEESE OMELETTE (3)
(Cheese, bread crumbs)

To 6 eggs add 2 tablespoons of grated Gruyère cheese, 2 tablespoons of cream, very little salt, a pinch of pepper, 2 tablespoons of crumbled stale bread, and 1 tablespoon of parsley, finely chopped. Beat all together and make the omelette in the usual way. Sprinkle over the omelette before folding, 1 tablespoon of the cheese, which has been coarsely grated into thin slivers, and 2 tablespoons of bread crumbs browned in 1 tablespoon of butter. Fold out on the platter and serve.

CHEESE   CHEESE OMELETTE MOUSSELINE (4)
(Cheese, bread crumbs, cream)

Soak ½ cup of bread crumbs in ½ cup of cream until the
cream has been absorbed. Beat separately the yolks and whites
of 4 eggs and add the creamy bread crumbs to the yolks, together with salt, pepper, and 3 tablespoons of grated Gruyère
cheese. Beat well together and fold in the stiffly beaten whites.
Cook in a generous amount of butter as an Omelette Mousseline (see page 21), fold one half over the other, slide out of
the pan, and serve.

CHEESE   CHEESE OMELETTE (5)
(Mozzarella cheese, bread croutons)

This is an Italian cheese omelette, or *frittata,* cooked on both
sides and served flat and not folded. Put 2 heaping tablespoons of butter in a pan and when melted, add 2 slices of
bread which have been cut in small cubes. Turn until brown
on all sides. Beat 4 eggs with ¼ pound of Mozzarella cheese,
diced, and a little salt and pepper. Pour the egg mixture over
the bread croutons and butter and cook over a low fire for
about 5 minutes. Turn the omelette out on a platter, as in the
directions for a *frittata* (see page 23), add a little more butter
to the pan if necessary, and slide the omelette back to finish
cooking on the other side.

CHEESE   ITALIAN RICOTTA OMELETTE
(Ricotta cheese, Parmesan cheese, tomato sauce)

Blend 2 tablespoons of flour and 1 tablespoon of water until
smooth. Beat 4 eggs and a pinch of salt with a fork for 30
seconds and mix well into the flour paste. Melt a little butter

in your smallest omelette pan and pour in 3 tablespoons of the egg mixture. Cook briefly on each side until set. Repeat this process until all the eggs have been used, spreading the little omelettes flat in a warm place.

Mix ½ pound of Ricotta, which is an Italian white pot cheese resembling cottage cheese, with 2 tablespoons of warm water, a pinch of salt, and 1 teaspoon of grated Parmesan cheese. Spread some of the cheese in the center of each little omelette, roll them up, place on a warm platter, and surround with tomato sauce (see page 175).

CHEESE   CHEESE FONDANT OMELETTE
(Swiss and Parmesan cheese custard)

Make a cheese cream as follows: break into a bowl 1 whole egg and 2 yolks. Beat and blend with 1 tablespoon of flour smoothed with ½ a cup of milk. Add salt and pepper, a pinch of cayenne, and 1 teaspoon of butter in a lump. Stir over the fire with a wooden spoon until it begins to thicken. Stir continuously to make it smooth and cook for 4 to 5 minutes. At the end, stir in ⅓ cup grated Swiss and Parmesan cheese combined.

Spread this cheese fondant in the center of a 6-egg omelette, fold out on a platter, sprinkle lightly with cheese, and surround with cream sauce (see page 172).

CHEESE   CHEESE TORTINO WITH TOMATOES
(Tomatoes, mint, cheese)

Peel, seed, and chop coarsely 3 large tomatoes and cook in 4 tablespoons of melted butter until soft and the liquid has evaporated. Flavor them with 1 teaspoon of chopped fresh mint, salt, and pepper. Beat 6 eggs lightly with salt and pepper and 2 tablespoons of grated Parmesan or Romano cheese.

Pour them over the tomatoes, stir all together, and cook until set. Serve from the pan.

COLD   OMELETTE CAMBACÉRÈS
(Foie gras, *rillette*, truffles, mayonnaise, ham, tomatoes)

✿ *This dish is wonderful for a cold buffet supper, and was named for a famous 20th century gastronome. It is particularly appealing when spread on a platter with a border of blue, or other harmonious color, to set off its rosy aspect.*

Make a 6-egg omelette in a pan large enough to spread the eggs rather thinly. When just cooked through, slide it out flat on a baking sheet or board to cool. Mix 3 tablespoons of purée of foie gras and 3 tablespoons of *rillette* (a kind of paté) of goose or pork. Spread this mixture over the whole surface of the omelette and roll it up on an oval platter. Coat the surface with a creamy, rather thin mayonnaise, colored and flavored with a little tomato ketchup. Place on top a row of sliced truffles, glazed with chicken aspic, and along each side an overlapping row of thin baked ham slices. As a finishing touch to this colorful dish heap at each end a mound of peeled, seeded, quartered tomatoes which have been well marinated in French dressing and then drained of all liquid. Place this dish in the refrigerator until ready to serve.

CURRY   CURRY OMELETTE
(Curry powder, seasonings)

Beat 6 eggs for an omelette with salt and pepper and ½ teaspoon of curry powder, or more, according to taste. Make the omelette in the usual way.

HONEY   HONEY OMELETTE OF APICIUS THE
ROMAN

(Honey, pepper)

✿ *This seems to be the first recorded omelette and is an*
indication of the venerable age of this dish. Apicius rec-
ommends the omelette baveuse, or slightly runny. As to
the pepper, use your own judgment. But this was the way
Apicius liked it.

Beat 4 eggs with one *hēmīna* of milk and one ounce of oil.
Heat a little oil in your earthen frying pan and pour in your
preparation. Turn out on a round dish before it is quite
cooked, spread with honey, sprinkle with freshly ground pepper and serve.

(As to the *hēmīna* of milk and ounce of oil—we would advise
2 tablespoons of the former and 1 tablespoon of the latter.)

MACARONI   MACARONI OMELETTE

(Macaroni, tomato sauce, cheese)

Fresh cooked or leftover macaroni may be used for this omelette. In either case it must be wiped dry and cut into half-
inch pieces. Heat ¾ cup of the cooked macaroni in 1 tablespoon of butter, season with salt and pepper, a pinch of nutmeg, and 1 tablespoon of grated Parmesan or Swiss cheese.
Add 2 tablespoons of tomato sauce (see page 175) and fold
into the center of a 6-egg omelette. When folded out on the
platter, sprinkle with grated cheese and surround with tomato
sauce if desired.

MACARONI   MACARONI FRITTATA
(Macaroni, parsley, cheese, capers)

Beat 6 eggs lightly with salt and pepper and 3 teaspoons of
water. Heat in butter 1 cup of cooked macaroni cut in ½-inch
pieces. Add 1 teaspoon finely chopped parsley, 1 teaspoon
grated Parmesan cheese, and 1 teaspoon of capers. Mix all
with the eggs and cook the *frittata* in 2 tablespoons of butter.
Brown the top briefly under the broiler and serve.

MACARONI   NEAPOLITAN OMELETTE
(Spaghetti, parsley, Parmesan cheese)

❀   *Try this nourishing dish when you have some leftover*
    cooked spaghetti in the refrigerator.
Cut up 3 cups of leftover cooked spaghetti with its sauce and
mix it with 4 beaten eggs, salt and pepper, 1 tablespoon finely
chopped parsley, and 2 tablespoons grated Parmesan cheese.
Heat 2 tablespoons olive oil in the frying pan, pour in the
mixture, and cook over a low fire about 10 minutes on each
side, or until done.

MACARONI   NOODLE OMELETTE
(Fried noodles, cheese)

❀   *As Paul Reboux points out,* noodle *is the epithet hurled*
    by Paris taxi-drivers at each other to designate the in-
    significant and soggy moral fibre of the offending com-
    petitor. But the golden crispness of the noodles used in
    this omelette recipe is something else again!
Before boiling your noodles, break them into pieces and add a
spoonful of oil to the water when half cooked. This coats

them lightly and keeps them from sticking together. Drain the noodles and dry on a cloth. Take 1½ cups of these cooked noodles, well separated, and sprinkle with flour, shaking them about until evenly coated. Now sauté them in 2 tablespoons, or more, of hot butter, turning with a fork, until they are golden. Sprinkle with grated Parmesan cheese and fold into the center of an omelette cooked just to a creamy consistency. The contrast of textures is delicious! Very fine bread crumbs may be substituted for flour in cooking the noodles if you desire.

MULTICOLORED   OMELETTE TRICOLOR
(Spinach juice, tomato, cream)

⚘   *This entertaining dish consists of 3 small 2-egg ome-lettes, each of a different color, placed side by side, and slightly overlapping, on a round platter.*
To the eggs for one 2-egg omelette add 1 tablespoon of green spinach juice, to the next, 1 tablespoon of tomato paste. The third is made of 2 eggs combined with 1 tablespoon of cream to obtain a pale color. Or, if you prefer, make it with 2 egg whites alone and a fourth of 2 yolks. When placed in their varicolored pattern on the serving dish, pour around the edge a creamy tomato sauce, color of the dawn, made by combining thick tomato sauce with cream to thin and pale it.

PINE NUTS   OMELETTE WITH PINE NUTS
(Pine nuts)

⚘   *This omelette may be either salt or sweet.*
Chop finely 2 tablespoons of pine nuts and pound them in a mortar to make a paste. Combine them with the 6 eggs beaten for an omelette. In 1 tablespoon of butter sauté 1 or more

tablespoons of whole pine nuts until slightly golden in color. Sprinkle with a pinch of salt. Add a little more butter to the pan if necessary, pour in the eggs, stir once or twice, and make your omelette.

To make a dessert omelette of this dish, add less salt to the eggs, none to the nuts, and sprinkle vanilla-flavored sugar over the surface of the omelette before folding, as well as on top after folding onto the platter.

RICE   **RICE AND CURRY OMELETTE**
(Onion, curry, rice)

Chop 1 small onion fine and sauté until golden in 1 teaspoon of butter. Stir in 1 teaspoon of curry powder and cook for 2 minutes. Now add 3 tablespoons of cream and cook 1 minute longer. Add to 6 beaten eggs flavored only with salt and make the omelette. Before folding fill with rice cooked as follows: Wash ⅓ cup of rice, drain, and dry on a cloth. Fry the rice for several minutes in butter, stirring continuously. When the rice has taken on a pale-yellow color, add just enough hot chicken stock to cover, cover the pan, and simmer until the rice is cooked and the liquid all absorbed. The rice should not be too soft and the grains should remain separate. Pour a little curry sauce around the omelette and serve.

RICE   **RICE AND TOMATO OMELETTE**
(Rice, tomato sauce)

Fill a 6-egg omelette with rice cooked as for the Rice and Curry Omelette. Or, if using leftover cooked rice, fry it a few minutes in butter. Add 1 or 2 tablespoons of stock and cook until absorbed. Pour tomato sauce (see page 175) over the top and serve.

SAUERKRAUT   SAUERKRAUT OMELETTE WITH
HAM

(Sauerkraut, ham, brown meat sauce)

Fill a 6-egg omelette with steamed, well-drained sauerkraut. Place thin slices of hot boiled ham on top and surround with a small amount of brown meat sauce made of juices from a roast. Or, make this by browning 1 tablespoon of butter in a pan and stirring in ½ teaspoon of meat extract melted in 2 tablespoons of stock.

SIX LAYER   OMELETTE GALANTINE

(Ham, sweetbread, mushrooms, foie gras, truffles, Supreme sauce)

❧ *This dish is composed of six 3-egg omelettes arranged one upon the other like a layer cake. Upon each is spread a layer of filling, a small portion of which has been separately chopped rather fine and mixed with the eggs before cooking the omelette. Each filling contains a small amount of sauce of fairly thick consistency and the top one is covered with Supreme sauce (see page 174) instead of a filling. For each filling use about 5 tablespoons of the particular mixture, one of which goes into the eggs and four on the surface of the omelette.*

Sauté 5 tablespoons of diced ham in a little butter. Remove 1 tablespoon of ham and chop finely to add to the eggs. To the rest add ¼ teaspoon of flour and blend in 1 tablespoon of Madeira wine and 1 tablespoon of stock. Heat and reduce to thick consistency.

Dice 1 parboiled sweetbread and sauté in butter with 2 sliced mushrooms. Chop 1 tablespoon of this and add to the eggs.

Add 1 tablespoon of chicken stock and 1 tablespoon of cream to the rest and simmer till reduced to fairly thick consistency. Another filling consists of diced pâté de foie gras barely heated in butter.

The fourth is a matter of 1 or 2 sliced truffles heated in butter and with a little of the Madeira juices from the can added.

The fifth consists of ¼ pound of sliced mushrooms sautéed in butter, blended with ¼ teaspoon of flour and a little cream.

If 1 teaspoon of fried bread croutons, a few drops of cream, and ½ teaspoon of chopped parsley is added to the eggs for each omelette with its particular filling ingredient, the result will be all the finer. Needless to say, each filling must be tested for just the right amount of salt and pepper to give savor.

All the fillings should first be prepared, then as the omelettes are made, one by one, they are placed one on top of the other, the fillings between, and over all ¾ cup of Supreme sauce (see page 174) is poured.

SNAILS   BURGUNDY OMELETTE
(Snails, walnuts, garlic, parsley)

Heat together in 1 tablespoon of butter 6 or 8 cooked snails, the chopped meats of 3 walnuts, 1 chopped clove of garlic, 1 teaspoon of chopped parsley, salt, and pepper. Fold this mixture into the center of a 6-egg omelette.

SNAILS   OMELETTE ARLÉSIENNE
(Snails, tomato, garlic, mustard)

Beat 6 eggs with 1 tablespoon of tomato purée, salt, and pepper. Heat 8 or 10 cooked snails in a little olive oil and spread on the omelette before folding.

Boil 4 cloves of garlic until slightly soft, mash through a fine sieve, and put them in a small saucepan with salt and pepper, ½ teaspoon of French mustard, a little oil, chopped parsley, and a few drops of vinegar. Heat and blend and spread this mixture on top of the omelette after folding.

WALNUTS   IRAQ WALNUT OMELETTE
(Walnuts, currants, saffron, turmeric, chives, bread crumbs)

❊ *All the mystery of the East is embodied in this omelette. In fact, it will be a real guessing game for your guests to divine its ingredients.*

Add to 6 beaten eggs ¾ cup of walnuts, finely chopped, ⅓ cup of dried currants, ¼ teaspoon of saffron, ¼ teaspoon of turmeric powder, 2 tablespoons of chopped chives, 4 table-spoons of bread crumbs, salt, and pepper. Cook the omelette in 1 tablespoon of melted butter and when done on one side, add more butter to the pan if necessary and turn to cook lightly on the other side.

SAUCES

ANCHOVY BUTTER

Cream 2 tablespoons of sweet butter with 1¾ tablespoons of anchovy paste and a few drops of onion juice.

BÉARNAISE SAUCE

In an earthenware bowl mix 2 egg yolks with 2 tablespoons of cream, 1 tablespoon of tarragon vinegar, salt, and a few grains of cayenne pepper. Put the bowl over a saucepan of hot water on a low fire and heat very gradually, stirring with a whisk. When the eggs begin to thicken add, a bit at a time, 4 good tablespoons of butter, stirring continuously. Mix in 1 teaspoon each of chopped fresh tarragon and parsley. It is the tarragon that gives Béarnaise sauce its characteristic taste.
This recipe is not apt to turn, and the earthen bowl is far safer than the extreme heat of a metal saucepan.

CHINESE SAUCE
(for Eggs Foo Yung)

Blend 2 teaspoons of cornstarch and ½ teaspoon of sugar with 1 teaspoon of soya sauce and a few drops of water. When completely smooth, add gradually ¾ cup of hot chicken stock. Cook, stirring, until thickened.

CHOCOLATE SAUCE

Melt over gentle heat 1½ ounces semi-sweet chocolate with 1 tablespoon of water. Make a syrup by boiling ½ cup of sugar with ¼ cup of water and combine with the chocolate gradually. Stir in 1 generous teaspoon of butter. Serve warm.

CREAM SAUCE

(for ½ cup)

Melt 1 tablespoon butter, stir in 1 teaspoon of flour, and add gradually ½ cup of rich milk or thin cream. Season with salt and pepper. Simmer and stir with a sauce whisk until thickened.

CURRY SAUCE

Sauté 1 small chopped onion in 1 tablespoon of butter until soft and slightly browned. Stir in 1 teaspoon of flour, salt, freshly milled pepper, ¼ teaspoon of powdered ginger, and ½ to 1 teaspoon of curry powder (depending on desired strength). Add gradually ⅓ cup of hot stock. Simmer and stir until slightly reduced. Add ¼ cup of cream, reheat, and strain the sauce.

LOBSTER BUTTER

Steep crushed lobster shells in the top of a double boiler with butter and a few drops of water in the proportion of 2 tablespoons of shells to 1 tablespoon of butter. After 20 minutes pour through a fine strainer, lined with a cheesecloth, placed over a bowl. Then pour a small amount of boiling water over the shells in the strainer (still placed over the bowl) to remove all remaining butter. Place the bowl in the refrigerator to chill. The butter will harden on top and can be removed for immediate use or stored in a small jar in the refrigerator.

MADEIRA SAUCE

In a saucepan heat 1 tablespoon of butter until it begins to turn brown. Blend in 1 tablespoon of flour and continue to cook, stirring, until the whole is a light nut-brown color. Stir in 1½ cups of good stock, bring to a boil, and then lower the heat to simmer until reduced by about half. Taste this for seasoning and add salt, or freshly ground pepper, if necessary. At the end add ¼ cup of Madeira wine and reheat to the boiling point, but do not allow the perfume of the fine Madeira wine to dissipate by overcooking.

MAÎTRE D'HÔTEL BUTTER

Heat 2 tablespoons of butter until it turns a light nut-brown, add juice of half a lemon, a pinch of salt and pepper, and a good teaspoon of finely chopped parsley.

MORNAY SAUCE

Make as Cream Sauce (see page 172), but add 1 tablespoon of grated Swiss and Parmesan cheese combined.

NANTUA SAUCE

(for ½ cup)

Melt 1 tablespoon lobster butter, blend in ¾ tablespoon flour, 1 tablespoon tomato paste, ½ cup cream, salt, and pepper. Stir and cook till slightly thickened.

NORMANDE SAUCE

(for ½ cup)

Blend 1½ teaspoons flour into 1½ teaspoons melted butter, add a pinch each of salt, pepper, and nutmeg, stir in a few drops of lemon juice, 3 tablespoons cider (or dry white wine), and ⅓ cup heavy cream. Cook, stirring, until thickened.

PÉRIGORD SAUCE

Melt 1 tablespoon of butter and add to it 2 chopped shallots and ½ an onion, chopped, and cook until lightly browned. Blend in 1 teaspoon of flour, salt, and pepper and let it take on a little color. Moisten with 1 tablespoon of stock and add ¾ cup of warmed white wine and 1 tablespoon of flamed brandy. Simmer, stirring often until somewhat reduced. Now strain the sauce through a sieve into another small pan, add 2 diced truffles, or truffle parings, and simmer together for 2 minutes. Stir in ½ teaspoon of meat extract or a little concentrated juice from roast meat. Skim off excess fat and serve.

SUPREME SAUCE

Blend 1 tablespoon butter with 1 heaping teaspoon flour, salt, and pepper and stir in gradually ¾ cup of liquid composed of half chicken stock and half heavy cream.

TOMATO SAUCE

(for ½ cup)

Melt 1 tablespoon of butter in a small pan, blend in 1 tea-spoon of flour, and add gradually 2 generous tablespoons to-mato paste and ⅓ cup stock.

FRESH TOMATO SAUCE

Sauté 1 small chopped onion in 1 tablespoon of butter until slightly browned, add salt and pepper, ½ teaspoon chopped fresh marjoram (or a good pinch of dried marjoram), a good pinch of thyme, 1 teaspoon chopped parsley, ½ clove of garlic, chopped, and 3 large peeled, coarsely chopped to-matoes. Add ½ cup of hot stock or water, cover, and simmer slowly for ½ hour or more, or until reduced to a good con-sistency. Force through a coarse sieve.

A NOTE ON THE TYPE

This book is set in Garamond, a modern rendering of the type first cut in the sixteenth century by Claude Garamond (1510–1561). He was a pupil of Geoffroy Tory and is believed to have based his letters on the Venetian models, although he introduced a number of important differences, and it is to him that we owe the letter which we know as Old Style. He gave to his letters a certain elegance and a feeling of movement which won for their creator an immediate reputation and the patronage of the French King, Francis I.

DESIGNED BY HARRY FORD